Fernand F. Hall, M.D.
77 West 55th St
NYC   10 April 1981

COLLECTED
POEMS

Marianne Moore

THE 100 GREATEST MASTERPIECES
OF AMERICAN LITERATURE
a limited edition collection
is published under the auspices of
The American Revolution
Bicentennial Administration

COLLECTED
POEMS

Marianne Moore

With an Introduction by T. S. Eliot

Illustrated by
Robert Andrew Parker

A Limited Edition

The Franklin Library
Franklin Center, Pennsylvania
1981

To
MARY WARNER MOORE
1862–1947

✣ Contents ✣

WHAT ARE YEARS? 1941

NEVERTHELESS, 1944

HITHERTO UNCOLLECTED

INTRODUCTION

WE KNOW VERY LITTLE ABOUT THE VALUE of the work of our contemporaries, almost as little as we know about our own. It may have merits which exist only for contemporary sensibility; it may have concealed virtues which will only become apparent with time. How it will rank when we are all dead authors ourselves we cannot say with any precision. If one is to talk about one's contemporaries at all, therefore, it is important to make up our minds as to what we can affirm with confidence, and as to what must be a matter of doubting conjecture. The last thing, certainly, that we are likely to know about them is their 'greatness', or their relative distinction or triviality in relation to the standard of 'greatness'. For in greatness are involved moral and social relations, relations which can only be perceived from a remoter perspective, and which may be said even to be created in the process of history: we cannot tell, in advance, what any poetry is going to do, how it will operate upon later generations. But the *genuineness* of poetry is something which we have some warrant for believing that a small number, but only a small number, of contemporary readers can recognise. I say positively only a small number, because it seems probable that when any poet conquers a really large public in his lifetime, an increasing proportion of his admirers will admire him for extraneous reasons. Not necessarily for bad reasons, but because he becomes known merely as a symbol, in giving a kind of stimulation, or consolation, to his readers, which is a function of his peculiar relation to them in time. Such effect upon contemporary readers may be a legitimate and proper result of some great poetry, but it has been also the result of much ephemeral poetry.

It does not seem to matter much whether one has to struggle with an age which is unconscious and self-satisfied, and therefore hostile to new forms of poetry, or with one like the present which is self-conscious and distrustful of itself, and avid for new forms which will give it status and self-respect. For many modern readers any superficial novelty of form is evidence of, or is as good as, newness of sensibility; and if the sensibility is fundamentally dull and second-hand, so much the better; for there is no quicker way of catching an immediate, if transient, popularity, than to serve stale goods in new packages. One of the tests—though it be only a negative test—of anything really new and genuine, seems to be its capacity for exciting aversion among 'lovers of poetry'.

I am aware that prejudice makes me underrate certain authors: I see them rather as public enemies than as subjects for criticism; and I dare say that a different prejudice makes me uncritically favourable to others. I may even admire the right authors for the wrong reasons. But I am much more confident of my appreciation of the authors whom I admire, than of my depreciation of the authors who leave me cold or who exasperate me. And in asserting that what I call *genuineness* is a more important thing to recognise in a contemporary than *greatness,* I am distinguishing between his function while living and his function when dead. Living, the poet is carrying on that struggle for the maintenance of a living language, for the maintenance of its strength, its subtlety, for the preservation of quality of feeling, which must be kept up in every generation; dead, he provides standards for those who take up the struggle after him. Miss Moore is, I believe, one of those few who have done the language some service in my lifetime.

So far back as my memory extends, which is to the pages of *The Egoist* during the War, and of *The Little Review* and *The Dial* in the years immediately following, Miss Moore has no immediate poetic derivations. I cannot, therefore, fill up my pages with the usual account of influences and development. There is one early poem, *A Talisman,* not reprinted in the text of this volume, which I will quote in full here, because it suggests a slight influence of H. D.,* certainly of H. D. rather than of any other 'Imagist':

> Under a splintered mast
> Torn from the ship and cast
> Near her hull,
>
> A stumbling shepherd found
> Embedded in the ground,
> A sea-gull
>
> Of lapis-lazuli,
> A scarab of the sea,
> With wings spread—
>
> Curling its coral feet,
> Parting its beak to greet
> Men long dead.

The sentiment is commonplace, and I cannot see what a bird carved of *lapis-lazuli* should be doing with *coral* feet; but even

* Hilda Doolittle (1886–1961), an American poet, founded the Imagist movement with Ezra Pound in 1911.

here the cadence, the use of rhyme, and a certain authoritativeness of manner distinguish the poem. Looking at Miss Moore's poems of a slightly later period, I should say that she had taken to heart the repeated reminder of Mr. Pound: that poetry should be as well written as prose. She seems to have saturated her mind in the perfections of prose, in its precision rather than its purple; and to have found her rhythm, her poetry, her appreciation of the individual word, for herself.

The first aspect in which Miss Moore's poetry is likely to strike the reader is that of minute detail rather than that of emotional unity. The gift for detailed observation, for finding the exact words for some experience of the eye, is liable to disperse the atttention of the relaxed reader. The minutiae may even irritate the unwary, or arouse in them only the pleasurable astonishment evoked by the carved ivory ball with eleven other balls inside it, the full-rigged ship in a bottle, the skeleton of the crucifix-fish. The bewilderment consequent upon trying to follow so alert an eye, so quick a process of association, may produce the effect of some 'metaphysical' poetry. To the moderately intellectual the poems may appear to be intellectual exercises; only to those whose intellection moves more easily will they immediately appear to have emotional value. But the detail has always its service to perform to the whole. The similes are there for use; as the mussel-shell 'opening and shutting itself like an injured fan' (where *injured* has an ambiguity good enough for Mr. Empson),* the waves 'as formal as the scales on a fish'. They make us see the object more clearly, though we may not understand immediately why our attention has been called to this object, and though we may not immediately grasp its association with a number of other objects. So, in her amused and affectionate attention to animals—from the domestic cat, or 'to popularize the mule', to the most exotic strangers from the tropics, she suc-

---

* William Empson (1906–), British poet and critic.

ceeds at once in startling us into an unusual awareness of visual patterns, with something like the fascination of a high-powered microscope.

Miss Moore's poetry, or most of it, might be classified as 'descriptive' rather than 'lyrical' or 'dramatic'. Descriptive poetry is supposed to be dated to a period, and to be condemned thereby; but it is really one of the permanent modes of expression. In the eighteenth century—or say a period which includes *Cooper's Hill*, *Windsor Forest*, and Gray's *Elegy*—the scene described is a point of departure for meditations on one thing or another. The poetry of the Romantic Age, from Byron at his worst to Wordsworth at his best, wavers between the reflective and the evocative; but the description, the picture set before you, is always there for the same purpose. The aim of 'imagism', so far as I understand it, or so far as it had any, was to induce a peculiar concentration upon something visual, and to set in motion an expanding succession of concentric feelings. Some of Miss Moore's poems—for instance with animal or bird subjects—have a very wide spread of association. It would be difficult to say what is the 'subject-matter' of *The Jerboa*. For a mind of such agility, and for a sensibility so reticent, the minor subject, such as a pleasant little sand-coloured skipping animal, may be the best release for the major emotions. Only the pedantic literalist could consider the subject-matter to be trivial; the triviality is in himself. We all have to choose whatever subject-matter allows us the most powerful and most secret release; and that is a personal affair.

The result is often something that the majority will call frigid; for to feel things in one's own way, however intensely, is likely to look like frigidity to those who can only feel in accepted ways.

> The deepest feeling always shows itself in silence;
> not in silence, but restraint.

It shows itself in a control which makes possible the fusion of the ironic-conversational and the high-rhetorical, as

> I recall their magnificence, now not more magnificent
> than it is dim. It is difficult to recall the ornament,
>   speech, and precise manner of what one might
>   call the minor acquaintances twenty
>   years back. . . .
>   strict with tension, malignant
>   in its power over us and deeper
>   than the sea when it proffers flattery in exchange
>   for hemp,
>   rye, flax, horses, platinum, timber and fur.

As one would expect from the kind of activity which I have been trying to indicate, Miss Moore's versification is anything but 'free'. Many of the poems are in exact, and sometimes complicated formal patterns, and move with the elegance of a minuet. ('Elegance', indeed, is one of her certain attributes.) Some of the poems (e.g. *Marriage, An Octopus*) are unrhymed; in others (e.g. *Sea Unicorns and Land Unicorns*) rhyme or assonance is introduced irregularly; in a number of the poems rhyme is part of a regular pattern interwoven with unrhymed endings. Miss Moore's use of rhyme is in itself a definite innovation in metric.

In the conventional forms of rhyme the stress given by the rhyme tends to fall in the same place as the stress given by the sense. The extreme case, at its best, is the pentameter couplet of Pope. Poets before and after Pope have given variety, sometimes at the expense of smoothness, by deliberately separating the stresses, from time to time; but this separation—often effected simply by longer periods or more involved syntax—can hardly be considered as more than a deviation from the norm for the purpose of avoiding monotony. The tendency of some of the best contemporary poetry is of course to dispense with rhyme altogether; but some of those who do use it have used it here and there to make a pattern directly in contrast with the sense and rhythm pattern, to give a greater intricacy. Some of the internal rhyming of Hopkins is to the point. (Genuine or auditory internal rhyme must not be confused with false or visual internal rhyme. If a poem reads just as well when cut up so that all the rhymes fall at the end of lines, then the internal rhyme is false and only a typographical caprice, as in Oscar Wilde's *Sphynx*.) This rhyme, which forms a pattern *against* the metric and sense pattern of the poem, may be either heavy or light—that is to say, either *heavier* or *lighter* than the other pattern. The two kinds, heavy and light, have doubtless different uses which remain to be explored. Of the *light* rhyme Miss Moore is the greatest living master; and indeed she is the first, so far as I know, who has investigated its possibilities. It will be observed that the effect sometimes requires giving a word a slightly more analytical pronunciation, or stressing a syllable more than ordinarily:

al-

ways has been—at the antipodes from the init-
    ial great truths. 'Part of it was crawling, part of it
was about to crawl, the rest
    was torpid in its lair.' In the short-legged, fit-
ful advance. . . .

It is sometimes obtained by the use of articles as rhyme words:

an
injured fan.
    The barnacles which encrust the side
    of the wave, cannot hide . . .

the
turquoise sea
of bodies. The water drives a wedge . . .

In a good deal of what is sometimes (with an unconscious theological innuendo) called 'modernist' verse one finds either an excess or a defect of technical attention. The former appears in an emphasis upon words rather than things, and the latter in an emphasis upon things and an indifference to words. In either case, the poem is formless, just as the most accomplished sonnet, if it is an attempt to express matter unsuitable for sonnet form, is formless. But a precise fitness of form and matter mean also a balance between them: thus the form, the pattern movement, has a solemnity of its own (e.g. Shakespeare's songs), however light and gay the human emotion concerned; and a gaiety of its own, however serious or tragic the emotion. The choruses of Sophocles, as well as the songs of Shakespeare, have another concern besides the human action of which they are spectators, and without this other concern there is not poetry. And on the other hand, if you aim only at the poetry in poetry, there is no poetry either.

My conviction, for what it is worth, has remained unchanged for the last fourteen years: that Miss Moore's poems form part of the small body of durable poetry written in our time; of that small body of writings, among what passes for poetry, in which an original sensibility and alert intelligence and deep feeling have been engaged in maintaining the life of the English language.

The original suggestion was that I should make a selection, from both previously published and more recent poems. But Miss Moore exercised her own rights of proscription first, so drastically, that I have been concerned to preserve rather than abate. I have therefore hardly done more than settle the order of the contents. This book contains all that Miss Moore was willing to reprint from the volume *Observations* (The Dial Press, New York, 1924), together with the poems written since that date which she is willing to publish. *

                                                      T. S. Eliot
August, 1934.

* This Introduction was originally written for the first edition of Marianne Moore's *Selected Poems,* published in 1935. Although many years have passed since it first appeared, it remains especially appropriate to introduce Miss Moore's poetry in this volume as well. The Introduction is used by permission of Mrs. T. S. Eliot.

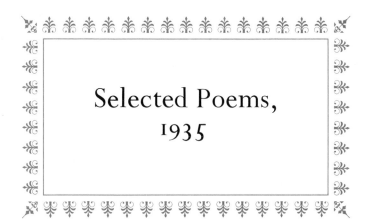

Selected Poems,
1935

❋ The Steeple-Jack

Dürer would have seen a reason for living
    in a town like this, with eight stranded whales
to look at; with the sweet sea air coming into your house
on a fine day, from water etched
    with waves as formal as the scales
on a fish.

One by one, in two's, in three's, the seagulls keep
    flying back and forth over the town clock,
or sailing around the lighthouse without moving their
    wings—
rising steadily with a slight
    quiver of the body—or flock
mewing where

a sea the purple of the peacock's neck is
    paled to greenish azure as Dürer changed
the pine green of the Tyrol to peacock blue and guinea
grey. You can see a twenty-five-
    pound lobster and fish-nets arranged
to dry. The

whirlwind fife-and-drum of the storm bends the salt
    marsh grass, disturbs stars in the sky and the
star on the steeple; it is a privilege to see so
much confusion.

      A steeple-jack in red, has let
    a rope down as a spider spins a thread;
he might be part of a novel, but on the sidewalk a
sign says C. J. Poole, Steeple-Jack,

3

in black and white; and one in red
and white says

Danger. The church portico has four fluted
columns, each a single piece of stone, made
modester by white-wash. This would be a fit haven for
waifs, children, animals, prisoners,
        and presidents who have repaid
sin-driven

senators by not thinking about them. One
        sees a school-house, a post-office in a
store, fish-houses, hen-houses, a three-masted schooner on
the stocks. The hero, the student,
        the steeple-jack, each in his way,
is at home.

It scarcely could be dangerous to be living
        in a town like this, of simple people
who have a steeple-jack placing danger-signs by the church
when he is gilding the solid-
        pointed star, which on a steeple
stands for hope.

✿ The Hero

Where there is personal liking we go.
   Where the ground is sour; where there are
   weeds of beanstalk height,
   snakes' hypodermic teeth, or
   the wind brings the 'scarebabe voice'
   from the neglected yew set with
   the semi-precious cat's eyes of the owl—
awake, asleep, 'raised ears extended to fine points', and so
on—love won't grow.

We do not like some things, and the hero
   doesn't; deviating head-stones
   and uncertainty;
   going where one does not wish
   to go; suffering and not
   saying so; standing and listening where something
   is hiding. The hero shrinks
as what it is flies out on muffled wings, with twin yellow
eyes—to and fro—

with quavering water-whistle note, low,
   high, in basso-falsetto chirps
   until the skin creeps.
   Jacob when a-dying, asked
   Joseph: Who are these? and blessed
   both sons, the younger most, vexing Joseph. And
   Joseph was vexing to some.
Cincinnatus was; Regulus; and some of our fellow
men have been, though

devout, like Pilgrim having to go slow
　　to find his roll; tired but hopeful—
　　hope not being hope
　　until all ground for hope has
　　vanished; and lenient, looking
　　upon a fellow creature's error with the
　　feelings of a mother—a
woman or a cat. The decorous frock-coated Negro
by the grotto

answers the fearless sightseeing hobo
　　who asks the man she's with, what's this,
　　what's that, where's Martha
　　buried, 'Gen-ral Washington
　　there; his lady, here'; speaking
　　as if in a play—not seeing her; with a
　　sense of human dignity
and reverence for mystery, standing like the shadow
of the willow.

Moses would not be grandson to Pharaoh.
　　It is not what I eat that is
　　my natural meat,
　　the hero says. He's not out
　　seeing a sight but the rock
　　crystal thing to see—the startling El Greco
　　brimming with inner light—that
covets nothing that it has let go. This then you may know
as the hero.

❧ The Jerboa

TOO MUCH

A Roman had an
artist, a freedman,
   contrive a cone—pine-cone
   or fir-cone—with holes for a fountain. Placed on
      the Prison of St. Angelo, this cone
      of the Pompeys which is known

now as the Popes', passed
for art. A huge cast
   bronze, dwarfing the peacock
   statue in the garden of the Vatican,
      it looks like a work of art made to give
      to a Pompey, or native

of Thebes. Others could
build, and understood
   making colossi and
   how to use slaves, and kept crocodiles and put
      baboons on the necks of giraffes to pick
      fruit, and used serpent magic.

They had their men tie
hippopotami
   and bring out dapple dog-
   cats to course antelopes, dikdik, and ibex;
      or used small eagles. They looked on as theirs,
      impalas and onigers,

the wild ostrich herd
with hard feet and bird

necks rearing back in the
dust like a serpent preparing to strike, cranes,
   mongooses, storks, anoas, Nile geese;
   and there were gardens for these—

combining planes, dates,
limes, and pomegranates,
   in avenues—with square
   pools of pink flowers, tame fish, and small frogs. Besides
      yarns dyed with indigo, and red cotton,
      they had a flax which they spun

into fine linen
cordage for yachtsmen.
   These people liked small things;
   they gave to boys little paired playthings such as
      nests of eggs, ichneumon and snake, paddle
      and raft, badger and camel;

and made toys for them-
selves: the royal totem;
   and toilet-boxes marked
   with the contents. Lords and ladies put goose-grease
      paint in round bone boxes with pivoting
      lid incised with the duck-wing

or reverted duck-
head; kept in a buck
   or rhinoceros horn,
   the ground horn; and locust oil in stone locusts.
      It was a picture with a fine distance;
      of drought, and of assistance

in time, from the Nile
rising slowly, while
   the pig-tailed monkey on
   slab-hands, with arched-up slack-slung gait, and
       the brown
     dandy, looked at the jasmine two-leafed twig
     and bud, cactus-pads, and fig.

Dwarfs here and there, lent
to an evident
   poetry of frog greys,
   duck-egg greens, and egg-plant blues, a fantasy
     and a verisimilitude that were
     right to those with, everywhere,

power over the poor.
The bees' food is your
   food. Those who tended flower-
   beds and stables were like the king's cane in the
     form of a hand, or the folding bedroom
     made for his mother of whom

he was fond. Princes
clad in queens' dresses,
   calla or petunia
   white, that trembled at the edge, and queens in a
     king's underskirt of fine-twilled thread like silk-
     worm gut, as bee-man and milk-

maid, kept divine cows
and bees; limestone brows,
   and gold-foil wings. They made

basalt serpents and portraits of beetles; the
    king gave his name to them and he was named
    for them. He feared snakes, and tamed

Pharaoh's rat, the rust-
backed mongoose. No bust
    of it was made, but there
    was pleasure for the rat. Its restlessness was
        its excellence; it was praised for its wit;
        and the jerboa, like it,

a small desert rat,
and not famous, that
    lives without water, has
    happiness. Abroad seeking food, or at home
        in its burrow, the Sahara field-mouse
        has a shining silver house

of sand. O rest and
joy, the boundless sand,
    the stupendous sand-spout,
    no water, no palm-trees, no ivory bed,
        tiny cactus; but one would not be he
        who has nothing but plenty.

ABUNDANCE

Africanus meant
the conqueror sent
   from Rome. It should mean the
   untouched: the sand-brown jumping-rat—free-born; and
      the blacks, that choice race with an elegance
      ignored by one's ignorance.

Part terrestrial,
and part celestial,
   Jacob saw, cudgel staff
   in claw-hand—steps of air and air angels; his
      friends were the stones. The translucent mistake
      of the desert, does not make

hardship for one who
can rest and then do
   the opposite—launching
   as if on wings, from its match-thin hind legs, in
      daytime or at night; with the tail as a weight,
      undulated out by speed, straight.

Looked at by daylight,
the underside's white,
   though the fur on the back
   is buff-brown like the breast of the fawn-breasted
      bower-bird. It hops like the fawn-breast, but has
      chipmunk contours—perceived as

it turns its bird head—
the nap directed
  neatly back and blending
  with the ear which reiterates the slimness
    of the body. The fine hairs on the tail,
    repeating the other pale

markings, lengthen till
at the tip they fill
  out in a tuft—black and
  white; strange detail of the simplified creature,
    fish-shaped and silvered to steel by the force
    of the large desert moon. Course

the jerboa, or
plunder its food store,
  and you will be cursed. It
  honours the sand by assuming its colour;
    closed upper paws seeming one with the fur
    in its flight from a danger.

By fifths and sevenths,
in leaps of two lengths,
  like the uneven notes
  of the Bedouin flute, it stops its gleaning
    on little wheel castors, and makes fern-seed
    foot-prints with kangaroo speed.

Its leaps should be set
to the flageolet;
   pillar body erect
   on a three-cornered smooth-working Chippendale
      claw—propped on hind legs, and tail as third toe,
      between leaps to its burrow.

✤ Camellia Sabina

and the Bordeaux plum
from Marmande (France) in parenthesis with
A. G. on the base of the jar—Alexis Godillot—
unevenly blown beside a bubble that
is green when held up to the light; they
are a fine duet; the screw-top
    for this graft-grown briar-black bloom
on black-thorn pigeon's-blood,
    is, like Certosa, sealed with foil. Appropriate custom.

    And they keep under
glass also, camellias catalogued by
lines across the leaf. The French are a cruel race—willing
to squeeze the diner's cucumber or broil a
meal on vine-shoots. Gloria mundi
with a leaf two inches, nine lines
    broad, they have; and the smaller,
Camellia Sabina
    with amanita-white petals; there are several of her

    pale pinwheels, and pale
stripe that looks as if on a mushroom the
sliver from a beet-root carved into a rose were laid. 'Dry
the windows with a cloth fastened to a staff.
In the camellia-house there must be
no smoke from the stove, or dew on
    the windows, lest the plants ail,'
the amateur is told;
    'mistakes are irreparable and nothing will avail.'

The scentless nosegay
is thus formed in the midst of the bouquet
from bottles, casks and corks, for sixty-four million red
        wines
and twenty million white, which Bordeaux merchants
and lawyers 'have spent a great deal of
trouble' to select, from what was
        and what was not Bordeaux. A
food-grape, however—'born
        of nature and of art'—is true ground for the
                grape-holiday.

The food of a wild
mouse in some countries is wild parsnip—or sunflower—or
morning-glory-seed, with an occasional
grape. Underneath the vines of the Bolzano
grape of Italy, the Prince of Tails
might stroll. Does yonder mouse with a
        grape in its hand and its child
in its mouth, not portray
        the Spanish fleece suspended by the neck? In that
                well-piled

        larder above your
head, the picture of what you will eat is
looked at from the end of the avenue. The wire cage is
locked, but by bending down and studying the
roof, it is possible to see the
pantomime of Persian thought: the

gilded, too tight undemure
coat of gems unruined
   by the rain—each small pebble of jade that refused to
      mature,

   plucked delicately
off. Off jewelry not meant to keep Tom
Thumb, the cavalry cadet, on his Italian upland
meadow-mouse, from looking at the grapes beneath
the interrupted light from them, and
dashing round the *concours hippique*
   of the tent, in a flurry
of eels, scallops, serpents,
   and other shadows from the blue of the green canopy.

   The wine-cellar? No
It accomplishes nothing and makes the
soul heavy. The gleaning is more than the vintage,
      though the
history *de la Vigne et du vin* place a
mirabelle in the *bibliothèque*
unique depuis seventeen-ninety-seven.
   (Close the window,
says the Abbé Berlèse,
   for Sabina born under glass.) O generous Bolzano!

❧ No Swan So Fine

'No water so still as the
    dead fountains of Versailles'. No swan,
with swart blind look askance
and gondoliering legs, so fine
    as the chintz china one with fawn-
brown eyes and toothed gold
collar on to show whose bird it was.

Lodged in the Louis Fifteenth
    candelabrum-tree of cockscomb-
tinted buttons, dahlias,
sea-urchins, and everlastings,
    it perches on the branching foam
of polished sculptured
flowers—at ease and tall. The king is dead.

✤ The Plumet Basilisk

IN COSTA RICA

In blazing driftwood
   the green keeps showing at the same place;
as, intermittently, the fire-opal shows blue and green.
   In Costa Rica the true Chinese lizard face
is found, of the amphibious falling dragon, the living
      fire-work.

He leaps and meets his
   likeness in the stream and, king with king,
helped by his three-part plume along the back, runs on two
      legs,
   tail dragging; faints upon the air; then with a spring
dives to the stream-bed, hiding as the chieftain with gold
      body hid in

Guatavita Lake.
   He runs, he flies, he swims, to get to
his basilica—'the ruler of Rivers, Lakes, and Seas,
   invisible or visible', with clouds to do
as bid—and can be 'long or short, and also coarse or fine
      at pleasure'.

THE MALAY DRAGON

We have ours; and they
   have theirs. Ours has a skin feather crest;
theirs has wings out from the waist which is snuff-brown
      or sallow.

Ours falls from trees on water; theirs is the smallest
dragon that knows how to dive head-first from a tree-top
      to something dry.

Floating on spread ribs,
   the boat-like body settles on the
clamshell-tinted spray sprung from the nutmeg-tree—
      minute legs
   trailing half akimbo—the true divinity
of Malay. Among unfragrant orchids, on the unnutritious
      nut-

tree, *myristica*
   fragrans, the harmless god spreads ribs that
do not raise a hood. This is the serpent-dove peculiar
   to the East; that lives as the butterfly or bat
can, in a brood, conferring wings on what it grasps, as the
      air-plant does.

THE TUATERA

Elsewhere, sea lizards—
   congregated so there is not room
to step, with tails laid criss-cross, alligator-style, among
   birds toddling in and out—are innocent of whom
they neighbour. Bird-reptile social life is pleasing. The
      tuatera

will tolerate a
   petrel in its den, and lays ten eggs
or nine—the number laid by dragons since 'a true dragon

has nine sons'. The frilled lizard, the kind with no legs,
and the three-horned chameleon, are non-serious ones that
      take to flight

if you do not. In
    Copenhagen the principal door
of the bourse is roofed by two pairs of dragons standing on
    their heads—twirled by the architect—so that the four
green tails conspiring upright, symbolize four-fold security.
      Now,

IN COSTA RICA

where sapotans drop
    their nuts out on the stream, there is, as
I have said, one of the quickest lizards in the world—the
    basilisk—that feeds on leaves and berries and has
shade from palm-vines, ferns, and peperomias; or lies basking
      on a

horizontal branch
    from which sour-grass and orchids sprout. If
best, he lets go, smites the water, and runs on it—a thing
    difficult for fingered feet. But when captured—stiff
and somewhat heavy, like fresh putty on the hand—he is
      no longer

the slight lizard that
    can stand in a receding flattened
S—small, long and vertically serpentine or, sagging,
    span the bushes in a fox's bridge. Vines suspend

the weight of something's shadow fixed on silk. By the
        Chinese brush, eight green

bands are painted on
    the tail—as piano keys are barred
by five black stripes across the white. This octave of faulty
    decorum hides the extraordinary lizard
till night-fall, which is for man the basilisk whose look will
        kill; but is

for lizards men can
    kill, the welcome dark—with the galloped
ground-bass of the military drum, the squeak of bag-pipes
    and of bats. Hollow whistled monkey-notes disrupt
the castanets. Taps from the back of the bow sound odd on
        last year's gourd,

or when they touch the
    kettledrums—at which, for there's no light,
a scared frog screaming like a bird, leaps out from weeds in
        which
    it could have hid, with curves of the meteorite,

            wide water-bug strokes,
        in jerks which express
        a regal and excellent awkwardness,

            the plumet portrays
        mythology's wish
        to be interchangeably man and fish—

travelling rapidly upward, as
spider-clawed fingers can twang the
bass strings of the harp, and with steps
as articulate, make their way
back to retirement on strings that
vibrate till the claws are spread flat.

    Among tightened wires,
minute noises swell
and change as in the woods' acoustic shell

    they will, with trees as
avenues of steel
to veil invisibleness ears must feel—

    black opal emerald opal
emerald—the prompt-delayed loud-
low chromatic listened-for down-
scale which Swinburne called in prose, the
noiseless music that hangs about
the serpent when it stirs or springs.

No anonymous
    nightingale sings in a swamp, fed on
sound from porcupine-quilled palm-trees blurring at the
       edge, that
    rattle like the rain. This is our Tower-of-London
jewel that the Spaniards failed to see, among the feather
       capes and hawk's-

head moths and black-chinned
    humming-birds; the innocent, rare, gold-
defending dragon that as you look begins to be a
    nervous naked sword on little feet, with three-fold
separate flame above the hilt, inhabiting fringe equidistant

from itself, of white
    fire eating into air. Thus nested
in the phosphorescent alligator that copies each
    digression of the shape, he pants and settles—head
up and eyes black as the molested bird's, with look of
        whetted fierceness,

in what is merely
    breathing and recoiling from the hand.
Thinking himself hid among the yet unfound jade
        axe-heads,
    silver jaguars and bats, and amethysts and
polished iron, gold in a ten-ton chain, and pearls the size of
        pigeon-eggs,

he is alive there
    in his basilisk cocoon beneath
the one of living green; his quicksilver ferocity
    quenched in the rustle of his fall into the sheath
which is the shattering sudden splash that marks his
        temporary loss.

❊ The Frigate Pelican

Rapidly cruising or lying on the air there is a bird
  that realizes Rasselas's friend's project
    of wings uniting levity with strength. This
       hell-diver, frigate-bird, hurricane-
bird; unless swift is the proper word
     for him, the storm omen when
    he flies close to the waves, should be seen
     fishing, although oftener
      he appears to prefer

to take, on the wing, from industrious crude-winged species
  the fish they have caught, and is seldom successless.
  A marvel of grace, no matter how fast his
    victim may fly or how often may
turn. The others with similar ease,
   slowly rising once more,
     move out to the top
     of the circle and stop

and blow back, allowing the wind to reverse their
       direction —
  Unlike the more stalwart swan that can ferry the
  woodcutter's two children home. Make hay; keep
    the shop; I have one sheep; were a less
limber animal's mottoes. This one
    finds sticks for the swan's-down-dress
    of his child to rest upon and would
     not know Gretel from Hänsel.
     As impassioned Handel —

meant for a lawyer and a masculine German domestic
   career—clandestinely studied the harpsichord
   and never was known to have fallen in love,
     the unconfiding frigate-bird hides
in the height and in the majestic
     display of his art. He glides
   a hundred feet or quivers about
        as charred paper behaves—full
     of feints; and an eagle

of vigilance. . . . *Festina lente.* Be gay
   civilly? How so? 'If I do well I am blessed
   whether any bless me or not, and if I do
     ill I am cursed.' We watch the moon rise
on the Susquehanna. In his way,
     this most romantic bird flies
   to a more mundane place, the mangrove
        swamp to sleep. He wastes the moon.
     But he, and others, soon

rise from the bough and though flying, are able to foil the
     tired
   moment of danger that lays on heart and lungs the
   weight of the python that crushes to powder.

❧ The Buffalo

     Black in blazonry means
prudence; and niger, unpropitious. Might
hematite—
     black, compactly incurved horns on bison
          have significance? The
     soot-brown tail-tuft on
          a kind of lion-

     tail; what would that express?
And John Steuart Curry's Ajax pulling
grass—no ring
     in his nose—two birds standing on the back?

          .   .   .   .   .   .

     The modern
ox does not look like the Augsburg ox's
portrait. Yes,
     the great extinct wild aurochs was a beast
          to paint, with stripe and six-
     foot horn-spread—decreased
          to Siamese-cat—

     Brown Swiss size or zebu-
shape, with white plush dewlap and warm-blooded
hump; to red-
     skinned Hereford or to piebald Holstein. Yet
          some would say the sparse-haired
     buffalo has met
          human notions best—

unlike the elephant,
both jewel and jeweller in the hairs
that he wears—
    no white-nosed Vermont ox yoked with its twin
      to haul the maple-sap,
    up to their knees in
      snow; no freakishly

Over-Drove Ox drawn by
Rowlandson, but the Indian buffalo,
albino-
    footed, standing in a mud-lake with a
      day's work to do. No white
    Christian heathen, way-
      laid by the Buddha,

    serves him so well as the
buffalo—as mettlesome as if check-
reined—free neck
    stretching out, and snake tail in a half-twist
      on the flank; nor will so
    cheerfully assist
      the Sage sitting with

    feet at the same side, to
dismount at the shrine; nor are there any
ivory
    tusks like those two horns which when a tiger
      coughs, are lowered fiercely
    and convert the fur
      to harmless rubbish.

The Indian buffalo,
led by bare-leggèd herd-boys to a hay
hut where they
    stable it, need not fear comparison
      with bison, with the twins,
   indeed with any
        of ox ancestry.

❧ Nine Nectarines

Arranged by two's as peaches are,
at intervals that all may live—
    eight and a single one, on twigs that
    grew the year before—they look like
a derivative;
    although not uncommonly
the opposite is seen—
nine peaches on a nectarine.
    Fuzzless through slender crescent leaves
        of green or blue or
        both, in the Chinese style, the four

pairs' half-moon leaf-mosaic turns
out to the sun the sprinkled blush
    of puce-American-Beauty pink
    applied to bees-wax grey by the
unenquiring brush
    of mercantile bookbinding.
Like the peach *Yu,* the red-
cheeked peach which cannot aid the dead,
    but eaten in time prevents death,
        the Italian
        peach-nut, Persian plum, Ispahan

secluded wall-grown nectarine,
as wild spontaneous fruit was
    found in China first. But was it wild?
    Prudent de Candolle would not say.
One perceives no flaws
    in this emblematic group
of nine, with leaf window

unquilted by *curculio*
    which someone once depicted on
      this much-mended plate
      or in the also accurate

    unantlered moose or Iceland horse
or ass asleep against the old
    thick, low-leaning nectarine that is the
    colour of the shrub-tree's brownish
flower.

   .   .   .   .   .

    A Chinese 'understands
the spirit of the wilderness'
    and the nectarine-loving kylin
    of pony appearance—the long-
tailed or the tailless
    small cinnamon-brown, common
camel-haired unicorn
with antelope feet and no horn,
    here enamelled on porcelain.
      It was a Chinese
      who imagined this masterpiece.

❧ The Fish

wade
through black jade.
  Of the crow-blue mussel-shells, one keeps
  adjusting the ash-heaps;
    opening and shutting itself like

an
injured fan.
  The barnacles which encrust the side
  of the wave, cannot hide
    there for the submerged shafts of the

sun,
split like spun
  glass, move themselves with spotlight swiftness
  into the crevices—
    in and out, illuminating

the
turquoise sea
  of bodies. The water drives a wedge
  of iron through the iron edge
    of the cliff; whereupon the stars,

pink
rice-grains, ink-
  bespattered jelly-fish, crabs like green
  lilies, and submarine
    toadstools, slide each on the other.

All
external
 marks of abuse are present on this
 defiant edifice—
  all the physical features of

ac-
cident—lack
 of cornice, dynamite grooves, burns, and
 hatchet strokes, these things stand
  out on it; the chasm-side is

dead.
Repeated
 evidence has proved that it can live
 on what can not revive
  its youth. The sea grows old in it.

❧ In This Age of Hard Trying, Nonchalance Is Good and

'really, it is not the
    business of the gods to bake clay pots'. They did not
        do it in this instance. A few
      revolved upon the axes of their worth
    as if excessive popularity might be a pot;

they did not venture the
    profession of humility. The polished wedge
      that might have split the firmament
        was dumb. At last it threw itself away
    and falling down, conferred on some poor fool, a
          privilege.

'Taller by the length of
    a conversation of five hundred years than all
      the others', there was one, whose tales
        of what could never have been actual—
    were better than the haggish, uncompanionable drawl

of certitude; his by-
    play was more terrible in its effectiveness
      than the fiercest frontal attack.
        The staff, the bag, the feigned inconsequence
    of manner, best bespeak that weapon, self-protectiveness.

❧ To Statecraft Embalmed

There is nothing to be said for you. Guard
Your secret. Conceal it under your hard
  Plumage, necromancer.
     O
Bird, whose tents were 'awnings of Egyptian
Yarn', shall Justice' faint zigzag inscription—
  Leaning like a dancer—
     Show
The pulse of its once vivid sovereignty?
You say not, and transmigrating from the
  Sarcophagus, you wind
     Snow
Silence round us and with moribund talk,
Half limping and half-ladyfied, you stalk
  About. Ibis, we find
     No
Virtue in you—alive and yet so dumb.
Discreet behaviour is not now the sum
  Of statesmanlike good sense.
     Though
It were the incarnation of dead grace?
As if a death-mask ever could replace
  Life's faulty excellence!
     Slow
To remark the steep, too strict proportion
Of your throne, you'll see the wrenched distortion
  Of suicidal dreams
     Go

Staggering toward itself and with its bill
Attack its own identity, until
   Foe seems friend and friend seems
    Foe.

I, too, dislike it: there are things that are important beyond
         all this fiddle.
  Reading it, however, with a perfect contempt for it, one
         discovers in
  it after all, a place for the genuine.
    Hands that can grasp, eyes
    that can dilate, hair that can rise
      if it must, these things are important not because a

high-sounding interpretation can be put upon them but
         because they are
  useful. When they become so derivative as to become
         unintelligible,
  the same thing may be said for all of us, that we
    do not admire what
    we cannot understand: the bat
      holding on upside down or in quest of something to

eat, elephants pushing, a wild horse taking a roll, a tireless
         wolf under
  a tree, the immovable critic twitching his skin like a
         horse that feels a flea, the base-
  ball fan, the statistician—
    nor is it valid
      to discriminate against 'business documents and

school-books'; all these phenomena are important. One
         must make a distinction
  however: when dragged into prominence by half poets,
         the result is not poetry,

nor till the poets among us can be
   'literalists of
   the imagination'—above
     insolence and triviality and can present

for inspection, 'imaginary gardens with real toads in them',
        shall we have
  it. In the meantime, if you demand on the one hand,
  the raw material of poetry in
   all its rawness and
   that which is on the other hand
     genuine, you are interested in poetry.

✿ Pedantic Literalist

Prince Rupert's drop, paper muslin ghost,
   white torch—'with power to say unkind
things with kindness, and the most
     irritating things in the midst of love and
      tears', you invite destruction.

You are like the meditative man
   with the perfunctory heart; its
carved cordiality ran
     to and fro at first like an inlaid and royal
      immutable production;

Then afterward 'neglected to be
   painful, deluding him with
loitering formality',
     'doing its duty as if it did it not',
      presenting an obstruction

To the motive that it served. What stood
   erect in you has withered. A
little 'palm-tree of turned wood'
     informs your once spontaneous core in its
      immutable production.

There is a great amount of poetry in unconscious
    fastidiousness. Certain Ming
        products, imperial floor-coverings of coach-
wheel yellow, are well enough in their way but I have
           seen something
        that I like better—a
           mere childish attempt to make an imperfectly bal-
              lasted animal stand up,
          similar determination to make a pup
        eat his meat from the plate.

I remember a swan under the willows in Oxford,
    with flamingo-coloured, maple-
        leaflike feet. It reconnoitred like a battle-
ship. Disbelief and conscious fastidiousness were the
              staple
        ingredients in its
           disinclination to move. Finally its hardihood was
              not proof against its
          proclivity to more fully appraise such bits
        of food as the stream

bore counter to it; it made away with what I gave it
    to eat. I have seen this swan and
        I have seen you; I have seen ambition without
understanding in a variety of forms. Happening to stand
        by an ant-hill, I have
          seen a fastidious ant carrying a stick north, south,
             east, west, till it turned on
          itself, struck out from the flower-bed into the
            lawn,
          and returned to the point

from which it had started. Then abandoning the stick as
    useless and overtaxing its
        jaws with a particle of whitewash—pill-like but
heavy, it again went through the same course of
                procedure.
                What is
        there in being able
            to say that one has dominated the stream in an
                attitude of self-defence;
            in proving that one has had the experience
                of carrying a stick?

winked too much and were afraid of snakes. The zebras,
                supreme in
their abnormality; the elephants with their fog-coloured
                skin
  and strictly practical appendages
    were there, the small cats; and the parrakeet—
      trivial and humdrum on examination, destroying
    bark and portions of the food it could not eat.

I recall their magnificence, now not more magnificent
than it is dim. It is difficult to recall the ornament,
  speech, and precise manner of what one might
    call the minor acquaintances twenty
      years back; but I shall not forget him—that
        Gilgamesh among
    the hairy carnivora—that cat with the

wedge-shaped, slate-grey marks on its forelegs and the
              resolute tail,
astringently remarking, 'They have imposed on us with
              their pale
  half-fledged protestations, trembling about
    in inarticulate frenzy, saying
      it is not for us to understand art; finding it
    all so difficult, examining the thing

as if it were inconceivably arcanic, as symmetrically frigid as if it had been carved out of chrysoprase
   or marble—strict with tension, malignant
      in its power over us and deeper
         than the sea when it proffers flattery in exchange for
            hemp,
      rye, flax, horses, platinum, timber, and fur.'

❧ Melanchthon

Openly, yes,
with the naturalness
   of the hippopotamus or the alligator
   when it climbs out on the bank to experience the

sun, I do these
things which I do, which please
   no one but myself. Now I breathe and now I am submerged; the blemishes stand up and shout when the
      object

in view was a
renaissance; shall I say
   the contrary? The sediment of the river which
   encrusts my joints, makes me very grey but I am used

to it, it may
remain there; do away
   with it and I am myself done away with, for the
   patina of circumstance can but enrich what was

there to begin
with. This elephant-skin
   which I inhabit, fibred over like the shell of
   the cocoanut, this piece of black glass through which no
      light

can filter—cut
into checkers by rut
   upon rut of unpreventable experience—
   it is a manual for the peanut-tongued and the

hairy-toed. Black
but beautiful, my back
    is full of the history of power. Of power? What
    is powerful and what is not? My soul shall never

be cut into
by a wooden spear; through-
    out childhood to the present time, the unity of
    life and death has been expressed by the circumference

described by my
trunk; nevertheless I
    perceive feats of strength to be inexplicable after
    all; and I am on my guard; external poise, it

has its centre
well nurtured—we know
    where—in pride; but spiritual poise, it has its centre
        where?
    My ears are sensitized to more than the sound of

the wind. I see
and I hear, unlike the
    wandlike body of which one hears so much, which was
        made
    to see and not to see; to hear and not to hear;

that tree-trunk without
roots, accustomed to shout
    its own thoughts to itself like a shell, maintained intact
    by who knows what strange pressure of the atmosphere;
        that

spiritual
brother to the coral-
    plant, absorbed into which, the equable sapphire light
    becomes a nebulous green. The I of each is to

the I of each
a kind of fretful speech
    which sets a limit on itself; the elephant is
    black earth preceded by a tendril? Compared with those

phenomena
which vacillate like a
    translucence of the atmosphere, the elephant is
    that on which darts cannot strike decisively the first

time, a substance
needful as an instance
    of the indestructibility of matter; it
    has looked at electricity and at the earth-

quake and is still
here; the name means thick. Will
    depth be depth, thick skin be thick, to one who can see
        no
    beautiful element of unreason under it?

✼ In the Days of Prismatic Colour

not in the days of Adam and Eve, but when Adam
   was alone; when there was no smoke and colour was
fine, not with the refinement
   of early civilization art, but because
of its originality; with nothing to modify it but the

mist that went up, obliqueness was a varia-
   tion of the perpendicular, plain to see and
to account for: it is no
   longer that; nor did the blue-red-yellow band
of incandescence that was colour keep its stripe: it also is
      one of

those things into which much that is peculiar can be
   read; complexity is not a crime, but carry
it to the point of murki-
   ness and nothing is plain. Complexity,
moreover, that has been committed to darkness, instead of
      granting it-

self to be the pestilence that it is, moves all a-
   bout as if to bewilder us with the dismal
fallacy that insistence
   is the measure of achievement and that all
truth must be dark. Principally throat, sophistication is as
      it al-

ways has been—at the antipodes from the init-
   ial great truths. 'Part of it was crawling, part of it
was about to crawl, the rest
   was torpid in its lair.' In the short-legged, fit-
ful advance, the gurgling and all the minutiae—we have
         the classic

multitude of feet. To what purpose! Truth is no Apollo
   Belvedere, no formal thing. The wave may go over it if it
         likes.
Know that it will be there when it says,
   'I shall be there when the wave has gone by.'

❀ Peter

Strong and slippery, built for the midnight grass-party
    confronted by four cats,
  he sleeps his time away—the detached first claw on the
    foreleg, which corresponds
to the thumb, retracted to its tip; the small tuft of fronds
  or katydid-legs above each eye, still numbering the
    units in each group;
    the shadbones regularly set about the mouth, to
    droop or rise

in unison like the porcupine's quills—motionless. He lets
    himself be flat-
tened out by gravity, as it were a piece of seaweed tamed
    and weakened by
exposure to the sun; compelled when extended, to lie
  stationary. Sleep is the result of his delusion that one
    must do as
    well as one can for oneself; sleep—epitome of what
    is to

him as to the average person, the end of life. Demonstrate
    on him how
the lady caught the dangerous southern snake, placing a
    forked stick on either
side of its innocuous neck; one need not try to stir
  him up; his prune-shaped head and alligator eyes are
    not a party to the
    joke. Lifted and handled, he may be dangled like an
    eel or set

up on the forearm like a mouse; his eyes bisected by pupils
    of a pin's
   width, are flickeringly exhibited, then covered up. May
     be? I should say
  might have been; when he has been got the better of in a
    dream—as in a fight with nature or with cats—we all
     know it. Profound sleep is
    not with him a fixed illusion. Springing about with
     froglike ac-

curacy, emitting jerky cries when taken in the hand, he is
    himself
  again; to sit caged by the rungs of a domestic chair
    would be unprofit-
able—human. What is the good of hypocrisy? It
   is permissible to choose one's employment, to abandon
    the wire nail, the
    roly-poly, when it shows signs of being no longer a
    pleas-

ure, to score the adjacent magazine with a double line of
    strokes. He can
  talk, but insolently says nothing. What of it? When one
    is frank, one's very
  presence is a compliment. It is clear that he can see
   the virtue of naturalness, that he is one of those who
    do not regard
    the published fact as a surrender. As for the
    disposition

invariably to affront, an animal with claws wants to have to use
   them; that eel-like extension of trunk into tail is not an accident. To
leap, to lengthen out, divide the air—to purloin, to pursue.
   To tell the hen: fly over the fence, go in the wrong way in your perturba-
      tion—this is life; to do less would be nothing but dishonesty.

❧ Picking and Choosing

Literature is a phase of life. If
   one is afraid of it, the situation is irremediable; if
one approaches it familiarly
   what one says of it is worthless. Words are constructive
when they are true; the opaque allusion—the simulated
     flight

upward—accomplishes nothing. Why cloud the fact
   that Shaw is self-conscious in the field of sentiment but is
     otherwise re-
warding; that James is all that has been
   said of him if feeling is profound? It is not Hardy
the distinguished novelist and Hardy the poet, but one man

'interpreting life through the medium of the
   emotions'. If he must give an opinion, it is permissible
     that the
critic should know what he likes. Gordon
   Craig with his 'this is I' and 'this is mine', with his three
wise men, his 'sad French greens' and his Chinese
     cherry—Gordon Craig, so

inclinational and unashamed—has carried
   the precept of being a good critic, to the last extreme,
     and Burke is a
psychologist—of acute, racoon-
   like curiosity. *Summa diligentia;*
to the humbug, whose name is so amusing—very young
     and very

rushed, Caesar crossed the Alps 'on the top of a
 diligence'. We are not daft about the meaning, but this
  familiarity
with wrong meanings puzzles one. Humming-
 bug, the candles are not wired for electricity.
Small dog, going over the lawn, nipping the linen and
  saying

that you have a badger—remember Xenophon;
 only the most rudimentary sort of behaviour is necessary
to put us on the scent; 'a right good
 salvo of barks', a few 'strong wrinkles' puckering the
skin between the ears, are all we ask.

✣ England

with its baby rivers and little towns, each with its abbey or
    its cathedral,
with voices—one voice perhaps, echoing through the
    transept—the
criterion of suitability and convenience: and Italy with its
    equal
shores—contriving an epicureanism from which the
    grossness has been

extracted: and Greece with its goat and its gourds, the nest
    of modified illusions:
and France, the 'chrysalis of the nocturnal butterfly', in
whose products mystery of construction diverts one from
    what was originally one's
object—substance at the core: and the East with its snails,
    its emotional

shorthand and jade cockroaches, its rock crystal and its
    imperturbability,
all of museum quality: and America where there
is the little old ramshackle victoria in the south, where
    cigars are smoked on the
street in the north; where there are no proof-readers, no
    silk-worms, no digressions;

the wild man's land; grassless, linksless, languageless
    country in which letters are written
not in Spanish, not in Greek, not in Latin, not in
    shorthand,

but in plain American which cats and dogs can read! The
     letter *a* in psalm and calm when
pronounced with the sound of *a* in candle, is very
     noticeable, but

why should continents of misapprehension have to be
     accounted for by the
fact? Does it follow that because there are poisonous
     toadstools
which resemble mushrooms, both are dangerous? In the
     case of mettlesomeness which may be
mistaken for appetite, of heat which may appear to be
     haste, no con-

clusions may be drawn. To have misapprehended the
     matter is to have confessed
that one has not looked far enough. The sublimated
     wisdom
of China, Egyptian discernment, the cataclysmic torrent of
     emotion compressed
in the verbs of the Hebrew language, the books of the man
     who is able

to say, 'I envy nobody but him, and him only, who catches
     more fish than
I do',—the flower and fruit of all that noted superi-
ority—should one not have stumbled upon it in America,
     must one imagine
that it is not there? It has never been confined to one
     locality.

✵ When I Buy Pictures

or what is closer to the truth,
when I look at that of which I may regard myself as the
        imaginary possessor,
I fix upon what would give me pleasure in my average
        moments:
the satire upon curiosity in which no more is discernible
than the intensity of the mood;
or quite the opposite—the old thing, the mediaeval
        decorated hat-box,
in which there are hounds with waists diminishing like the
        waist of the hour-glass,
and deer and birds and seated people;
it may be no more than a square of parquetry; the literal
        biography perhaps,
in letters standing well apart upon a parchment-like
        expanse;
an artichoke in six varieties of blue; the snipe-legged
        hieroglyphic in three parts;
the silver fence protecting Adam's grave, or Michael taking
        Adam by the wrist.
Too stern an intellectual emphasis upon this quality or that
        detracts from one's enjoyment.
It must not wish to disarm anything; nor may the approved
        triumph easily be honoured—
that which is great because something else is small.
It comes to this: of whatever sort it is,
it must be 'lit with piercing glances into the life of things';
it must acknowledge the spiritual forces which have made it.

A Grave

Man looking into the sea,
taking the view from those who have as much right to it as
    you have to it yourself,
it is human nature to stand in the middle of a thing,
but you cannot stand in the middle of this;
the sea has nothing to give but a well excavated grave.
The firs stand in a procession, each with an emerald
    turkey-foot at the top,
reserved as their contours, saying nothing;
repression, however, is not the most obvious characteristic
    of the sea;
the sea is a collector, quick to return a rapacious look.
There are others besides you who have worn that look—
whose expression is no longer a protest; the fish no longer
    investigate them
for their bones have not lasted:
men lower nets, unconscious of the fact that they are
    desecrating a grave,
and row quickly away—the blades of the oars
moving together like the feet of water-spiders as if there
    were no such thing as death.
The wrinkles progress among themselves in a phalanx—
    beautiful under networks of foam,
and fade breathlessly while the sea rustles in and out of the
    seaweed;
the birds swim through the air at top speed, emitting
    cat-calls as heretofore—
the tortoise-shell scourges about the feet of the cliffs, in
    motion beneath them;

and the ocean, under the pulsation of lighthouses and noise
    of bell-buoys,
advances as usual, looking as if it were not that ocean in
    which dropped things are bound to sink—
in which if they turn and twist, it is neither with volition
    nor consciousness.

✿ *Those Various Scalpels,*

those

various sounds consistently indistinct, like intermingled
    echoes
    struck from thin glasses successively at random—the
      inflection disguised: your hair, the tails of two
    fighting-cocks head to head in stone—like sculptured
      scimitars re-
        peating the curve of your ears in reverse order: your
        eyes, flowers of ice

and

snow sown by tearing winds on the cordage of disabled
    ships; your raised hand,
    an ambiguous signature: your cheeks, those rosettes
      of blood on the stone floors of French châteaux, with
    regard to which the guides are so affirmative—those
      regrets
      of the retoucher on the contemporary stone: your
      other hand,

a

bundle of lances all alike, partly hid by emeralds from
    Persia
    and the fractional magnificence of Florentine
      goldwork—a collection of little objects—
    sapphires set with emeralds, and pearls with a
      moonstone, made fine
      with enamel in grey, yellow, and dragon-fly blue; a
      lemon, a

pear
and three bunches of grapes, tied with silver: your dress, a
        magnificent square
    cathedral tower of uniform
        and at the same time, diverse appearance—a
    species of vertical vineyard rustling in the storm
        of conventional opinion. Are they weapons or
        scalpels? Whetted

to
brilliance by the hard majesty of that sophistication which
        is su-
    perior to opportunity, these things are rich
        instruments with which to experiment; naturally. But
    why dissect destiny with instruments which
        are more highly specialized than the tissues of destiny
        itself?

To popularize the mule, its neat exterior
expressing the principle of accommodation reduced to a
    minimum:
to persuade one of austere taste, proud in the possession of
    home and a musician—
that the piano is a free field for etching; that his 'charming
    tadpoles notes'
belong to the past when one had time to play them:
to persuade those self-wrought Midases of brains
whose fourteen carat ignorance aspires to rise in value
till the sky is the limit,
that excessive conduct augurs disappointment,
that one must not borrow a long white beard and tie it on
and threaten with the scythe of time the casually curious:
to teach the bard with too elastic a selectiveness
that one detects creative power by its capacity to conquer
    one's detachment,
that while it may have more elasticity than logic,
it knows where it is going;
it flies along in a straight line like electricity,
depopulating areas that boast of their remoteness,
to prove to the high priests of caste
that snobbishness is a stupidity,
the best side out, of age-old toadyism,
kissing the feet of the man above,
kicking the face of the man below;
to teach the patron-saints-to-atheists, the Coliseum
meet-me-alone-by-moonlight maudlin troubadour
that kickups for catstrings are not life
nor yet appropriate to death—that we are sick of the earth,
sick of the pig-sty, wild geese and wild men;

to convince snake-charming controversialists
that it is one thing to change one's mind,
another to eradicate it—that one keeps on knowing
'that the Negro is not brutal,
that the Jew is not greedy,
that the Oriental is not immoral,
that the German is not a Hun'.

✤ New York

the savage's romance,
accreted where we need the space for commerce—
the centre of the wholesale fur trade,
starred with tepees of ermine and peopled with foxes,
the long guard-hairs waving two inches beyond the body of
    the pelt;
the ground dotted with deer-skins—white with white
    spots,
'as satin needlework in a single colour may carry a varied
    pattern',
and wilting eagle's-down compacted by the wind;
and picardels of beaver-skin; white ones alert with snow.
It is a far cry from the 'queen full of jewels'
and the beau with the muff,
from the gilt coach shaped like a perfume-bottle,
to the conjunction of the Monongahela and the Allegheny,
and the scholastic philosophy of the wilderness
to combat which one must stand outside and laugh
since to go in is to be lost.
It is not the dime-novel exterior,
Niagara Falls, the calico horses and the war-canoe;
it is not that 'if the fur is not finer than such as one sees
    others wear,
one would rather be without it'—
that estimated in raw meat and berries, we could feed the
    universe;
it is not the atmosphere of ingenuity,
the otter, the beaver, the puma skins
without shooting-irons or dogs;
it is not the plunder,
but 'accessibility to experience'.

❦ People's Surroundings

They answer one's questions,
a deal table compact with the wall;
in this dried bone of arrangement
one's 'natural promptness' is compressed, not crowded out;
one's style is not lost in such simplicity.

The palace furniture, so old fashioned, so old fashionable;
Sèvres china and the fireplace dogs—
bronze dromios with pointed ears, as obsolete as pugs;
one has one's preferences in the matter of bad furniture,
and this is not one's choice.

The vast indestructible necropolis
of composite Yawman-Erbe separable units;
the steel, the oak, the glass, the Poor Richard publications
containing the public secrets of efficiency
on paper so thin that 'one thousand four hundred and
        twenty pages make one inch',
exclaiming, so to speak, When you take my time, you take
        something I had meant to use;

the highway hid by fir-trees in rhododendron twenty feet
        deep,
the peacocks, hand-forged gates, old Persian velvet,
roses outlined in pale black on an ivory ground,
the pierced iron shadows of the cedars,
Chinese carved glass, old Waterford,
lettered ladies; landscape gardening twisted into
        permanence;

straight lines over such great distances as one finds in Utah
    or in Texas,
where people do not have to be told
that a good brake is as important as a good motor;
where by means of extra sense-cells in the skin
they can, like trout, smell what is coming—
those cool sirs with the explicit sensory apparatus of
    common sense,
who know the exact distance between two points as the
    crow flies;
there is something attractive about a mind that moves in a
    straight line—
the municipal bat-roost of mosquito warfare, concrete
    statuary,
medicaments for instant beauty in the hands of all,
and that live wire, the American string quartette;
these are questions more than answers,

and Bluebeard's Tower above the coral-reefs,
the magic mouse-trap closing on all points of the compass,
capping like petrified surf the furious azure of the bay,
where there is no dust, and life is like a lemon-leaf,
a green piece of tough translucent parchment,
where the crimson, the copper, and the Chinese vermilion
    of the poincianas
set fire to the masonry and turquoise blues refute the clock;
this dungeon with odd notions of hospitality,
with its 'chessmen carved out of moonstones',
its mocking-birds, fringed lilies, and hibiscus,
its black butterflies with blue half circles on their wings,
tan goats with onyx ears, its lizards glittering and without
    thickness,

like splashes of fire and silver on the pierced turquoise of
    the lattices
and the acacia-like lady shivering at the touch of a hand,
lost in a small collision of the orchids—
dyed quicksilver let fall
to disappear like an obedient chameleon in fifty shades of
    mauve and amethyst.
Here where the mind of this establishment has come to the
    conclusion
that it would be impossible to revolve about oneself too
    much,
sophistication has, 'like an escalator', 'cut the nerve of
    progress'.

In these non-committal, personal-impersonal expressions of
    appearance,
the eye knows what to skip;
the physiognomy of conduct must not reveal the skeleton;
'a setting must not have the air of being one',
yet with X-ray-like inquisitive intensity upon it, the surfaces
    go back;
the interfering fringes of expression are but a stain on what
    stands out,
there is neither up nor down to it;
we see the exterior and the fundamental structure—
captains of armies, cooks, carpenters,
cutlers, gamesters, surgeons and armourers,
lapidaries, silkmen, glovers, fiddlers and ballad-singers,
sextons of churches, dyers of black cloth, hostlers and
    chimney-sweeps,
queens, countesses, ladies, emperors, travellers and
    mariners,

dukes, princes and gentlemen,
in their respective places—
camps, forges and battlefields,
conventions, oratories and wardrobes,
dens, deserts, railway stations, asylums and places where
    engines are made,
shops, prisons, brickyards and altars of churches—
in magnificent places clean and decent,
castles, palaces, dining-halls, theatres and imperial
    audience-chambers.

❧ Snakes, Mongooses, Snake-Charmers and the Like

I have a friend who would give a price for those long
    fingers all of one length—
those hideous bird's claws, for that exotic asp and the
    mongoose—
products of the country in which everything is hard work,
    the country of the grass-getter,
the torch-bearer, the dog-servant, the messenger-bearer, the
    holy-man.
Engrossed in this distinguished worm nearly as wild and as
    fierce as the day it was caught,
he gazes as if incapable of looking at anything with a view
    to analysis.
'The slight snake rippling quickly through the grass,
the leisurely tortoise with its pied back,
the chameleon passing from twig to stone, from stone to
    straw',
lit his imagination at one time; his admiration now
    converges upon this.
Thick, not heavy, it stands up from its travelling-basket,
the essentially Greek, the plastic animal all of a piece from
    nose to tail;
one is compelled to look at it as at the shadows of the alps
imprisoning in their folds like flies in amber, the rhythms of
    the skating rink.
This animal to which from the earliest times, importance
    has attached,
fine as its worshippers have said—for what was it
    invented?

To show that when intelligence in its pure form
has embarked on a train of thought which is unproductive,
    it will come back?
We do not know; the only positive thing about it is its
    shape; but why protest?
The passion for setting people right is in itself an afflictive
    disease.
Distaste which takes no credit to itself is best.

❧ Bowls

on the green
with lignum vitae balls and ivory markers,
the pins planted in wild duck formation,
and quickly dispersed—
by this survival of ancient punctilio
in the manner of Chinese lacquer-carving,
layer after layer exposed by certainty of touch and
     unhurried incision
so that only so much colour shall be revealed as is
     necessary to the picture,
I learn that we are precisionists,
not citizens of Pompeii arrested in action
as a cross-section of one's correspondence would seem to
     imply.
Renouncing a policy of boorish indifference
to everything that has been said since the days of Matilda,
I shall purchase an etymological dictionary of modern
     English
that I may understand what is written,
and like the ant and the spider
returning from time to time to headquarters,
shall answer the question
'why do I like winter better than I like summer?'
and acknowledge that it does not make me sick
to look playwrights and poets and novelists straight in the
     face—
that I feel just the same;
and I shall write to the publisher of the magazine
which will 'appear the first day of the month

and disappear before one has had time to buy it
unless one takes proper precaution',
and make an effort to please—
since he who gives quickly gives twice
in nothing so much as in a letter.

.

anatomize their work
in the sense in which Will Honeycomb was jilted by a
    duchess;
the little assumptions of the scared ego confusing the issue
so that they do not know 'whether it is the buyer or the
    seller who gives the money'—
an abstruse idea plain to none but the artist,
the only seller who buys, and holds on to the money.
Because one expresses oneself and entitles it wisdom, one is
    not a fool. What an idea!
'Dracontine cockatrices, perfect and poisonous from the
    beginning',
they present themselves as a contrast to sea-serpented
    regions 'unlit by the half-lights of more conscious art'.

Acquiring at thirty what at sixty they will be trying to
    forget,
blind to the right word, deaf to satire
which like 'the smell of the cypress strengthens the nerves
    of the brain',
averse from the antique
with 'that tinge of sadness about it which a reflective mind
    always feels,
it is so little and so much'—
they write the sort of thing that would in their judgment
    interest a lady;
curious to know if we do not adore each letter of the
    alphabet that goes to make a word of it—
according to the Act of Congress, the sworn statement of
    the treasurer and all the rest of it—

the counterpart to what we are:
stupid man; men are strong and no one pays any attention:
stupid woman; women have charm, and how annoying
 they can be.
Yes, 'the authors are wonderful people, particularly those
 that write the most',
the masters of all languages, the supertadpoles of
 expression.
Accustomed to the recurring phosphorescence of antiquity,
the 'much noble vagueness and indefinite jargon' of Plato,
the lucid movements of the royal yacht upon the learned
 scenery of Egypt—
king, steward, and harper, seated amidships while the jade
 and the rock crystal course about in solution,

their suavity surmounts the surf—
the willowy wit, the transparent equation of Isaiah,
 Jeremiah, Ezekiel, Daniel.
Bored by 'the detailless perspective of the sea', reiterative
 and naïve,
and its chaos of rocks—the stuffy remarks of the
 Hebrews—
the good and alive young men demonstrate the assertion
that it is not necessary to be associated with that which has
 bored one;
they have never made a statement which they found so easy
 to prove—
'split like a glass against a wall'
in this 'precipitate of dazzling impressions,
the spontaneous unforced passion of the Hebrew
 language—

an abyss of verbs full of reverberations and tempestuous
      energy'
in which action perpetuates action and angle is at variance
      with angle
till submerged by the general action;
obscured by 'fathomless suggestions of colour',
by incessantly panting lines of green, white with
      concussion,
in this drama of water against rocks—this 'ocean of
      hurrying consonants'
with its 'great livid stains like long slabs of green marble',
its 'flashing lances of perpendicular lightning' and 'molten
      fires swallowed up',
'with foam on its barriers',
'crashing itself out in one long hiss of spray'.

✿ Marriage

This institution,
perhaps one should say enterprise
out of respect for which
one says one need not change one's mind
about a thing one has believed in,
requiring public promises
of one's intention
to fulfil a private obligation:
I wonder what Adam and Eve
think of it by this time,
this fire-gilt steel
alive with goldenness;
how bright it shows—
'of circular traditions and impostures,
committing many spoils',
requiring all one's criminal ingenuity
to avoid!
Psychology which explains everything
explains nothing,
and we are still in doubt.
Eve: beautiful woman—
I have seen her
when she was so handsome
she gave me a start,
able to write simultaneously
in three languages—
English, German and French—
and talk in the meantime;
equally positive in demanding a commotion
and in stipulating quiet:

'I should like to be alone';
to which the visitor replies,
'I should like to be alone;
why not be alone together?'
Below the incandescent stars
below the incandescent fruit,
the strange experience of beauty;
its existence is too much;
it tears one to pieces
and each fresh wave of consciousness
is poison.
'See her, see her in this common world',
the central flaw
in that first crystal-fine experiment,
this amalgamation which can never be more
than an interesting impossibility,
describing it
as 'that strange paradise
unlike flesh, stones,
gold or stately buildings,
the choicest piece of my life:
the heart rising
in its estate of peace
as a boat rises
with the rising of the water';
constrained in speaking of the serpent—
shed snakeskin in the history of politeness
not to be returned to again—
that invaluable accident
exonerating Adam.

And he has beauty also;
it's distressing—the O thou
to whom from whom,
without whom nothing—Adam;
'something feline,
something colubrine'—how true!
a crouching mythological monster
in that Persian miniature of emerald mines,
raw silk—ivory white, snow white,
oyster white and six others—
that paddock full of leopards and giraffes—
long lemon-yellow bodies
sown with trapezoids of blue.
Alive with words,
vibrating like a cymbal
touched before it has been struck,
he has prophesied correctly—
the industrious waterfall,
'the speedy stream
which violently bears all before it,
at one time silent as the air
and now as powerful as the wind'.
'Treading chasms
on the uncertain footing of a spear',
forgetting that there is in woman
a quality of mind
which as an instinctive manifestation
is unsafe,
he goes on speaking
in a formal customary strain,
of 'past states, the present state,

seals, promises,
the evil one suffered,
the good one enjoys,
hell, heaven,
everything convenient
to promote one's joy'.
In him a state of mind
perceives what it was not
intended that he should;
'he experiences a solemn joy
in seeing that he has become an idol'.
Plagued by the nightingale
in the new leaves,
with its silence —
not its silence but its silences,
he says of it:
'It clothes me with a shirt of fire'.
'He dares not clap his hands
to make it go on
lest it should fly off;
if he does nothing, it will sleep;
if he cries out, it will not understand'.
Unnerved by the nightingale
and dazzled by the apple,
impelled by 'the illusion of a fire
effectual to extinguish fire',
compared with which
the shining of the earth
is but deformity — a fire
'as high as deep
as bright as broad

as long as life itself',
he stumbles over marriage,
'a very trivial object indeed'
to have destroyed the attitude
in which he stood—
the ease of the philosopher
unfathered by a woman.
Unhelpful Hymen!
a kind of overgrown cupid
reduced to insignificance
by the mechanical advertising
parading as involuntary comment,
by that experiment of Adam's
with ways out but no way in—
the ritual of marriage,
augmenting all its lavishness;
its fiddle-head ferns,
lotus flowers, opuntias, white dromedaries,
its hippopotamus—
nose and mouth combined
in one magnificent hopper—
its snake and the potent apple.
He tells us
that 'for love that will
gaze an eagle blind,
that is with Hercules
climbing the trees
in the garden of the Hesperides,
from forty-five to seventy
is the best age',
commending it

as a fine art, as an experiment,
a duty or as merely recreation.
One must not call him ruffian
nor friction a calamity—
the fight to be affectionate:
'no truth can be fully known
until it has been tried
by the tooth of disputation'.
The blue panther with black eyes,
the basalt panther with blue eyes,
entirely graceful—
one must give them the path—
the black obsidian Diana
who 'darkeneth her countenance
as a bear doth',
the spiked hand
that has an affection for one
and proves it to the bone,
impatient to assure you
that impatience is the mark of independence,
not of bondage.
'Married people often look that way'—
'seldom and cold, up and down,
mixed and malarial
with a good day and a bad'.
'When do we feed?'
We occidentals are so unemotional,
we quarrel as we feed;
self lost, the irony preserved
in 'the Ahasuerus *tête-à-tête* banquet'
with its small orchids like snakes' tongues,

with its 'good monster, lead the way',
with little laughter
and munificence of humour
in that quixotic atmosphere of frankness
in which, 'four o'clock does not exist,
but at five o'clock
the ladies in their imperious humility
are ready to receive you';
in which experience attests
that men have power
and sometimes one is made to feel it.
He says, 'What monarch would not blush
to have a wife
with hair like a shaving-brush?
The fact of woman
is "not the sound of the flute
but very poison"'.
She says, 'Men are monopolists
of "stars, garters, buttons
and other shining baubles"—
unfit to be the guardians
of another person's happiness'.
He says, 'These mummies
must be handled carefully—
"the crumbs from a lion's meal,
a couple of shins and the bit of an ear";
turn to the letter M
and you will find
that "a wife is a coffin",
that severe object
with the pleasing geometry

stipulating space not people,
refusing to be buried
and uniquely disappointing,
revengefully wrought in the attitude
of an adoring child
to a distinguished parent'.
She says, 'This butterfly,
this waterfly, this nomad
that has "proposed
to settle on my hand for life". —
What can one do with it?
There must have been more time
in Shakespeare's day
to sit and watch a play.
You know so many artists who are fools'.
He says, 'You know so many fools
who are not artists'.
The fact forgot
that 'some have merely rights
while some have obligations',
he loves himself so much,
he can permit himself
no rival in that love.
She loves herself so much,
she cannot see herself enough—
a statuette of ivory on ivory,
the logical last touch
to an expansive splendour
earned as wages for work done:
one is not rich but poor
when one can always seem so right.

What can one do for them—
these savages
condemned to disaffect
all those who are not visionaries
alert to undertake the silly task
of making people noble?
This model of petrine fidelity
who 'leaves her peaceful husband
only because she has seen enough of him'—
that orator reminding you,
'I am yours to command'.
'Everything to do with love is mystery;
it is more than a day's work
to investigate this science'.
One sees that it is rare—
that striking grasp of opposites
opposed each to the other, not to unity,
which in cycloid inclusiveness
has dwarfed the demonstration
of Columbus with the egg—
a triumph of simplicity—
that charitive Euroclydon
of frightening disinterestedness
which the world hates,
admitting:

> 'I am such a cow,
> if I had a sorrow
> I should feel it a long time;
> I am not one of those
> who have a great sorrow

in the morning
and a great joy at noon';

which says: 'I have encountered it
among those unpretentious
protégés of wisdom,
where seeming to parade
as the debater and the Roman,
the statesmanship
of an archaic Daniel Webster
persists to their simplicity of temper
as the essence of the matter:

"Liberty and union
now and forever";

the Book on the writing-table;
the hand in the breast-pocket'.

of ice. Deceptively reserved and flat,
it lies 'in grandeur and in mass'
beneath a sea of shifting snow-dunes;
dots of cyclamen-red and maroon on its clearly defined
    pseudo-podia
made of glass that will bend—a much needed invention—
comprising twenty-eight ice-fields from fifty to five
    hundred feet thick,
of unimagined delicacy.
'Picking periwinkles from the cracks'
or killing prey with the concentric crushing rigour of the
    python,
it hovers forward 'spider fashion
on its arms' misleadingly like lace;
its 'ghostly pallor changing
to the green metallic tinge of an anemone-starred pool'.
The fir-trees, in 'the magnitude of their root systems',
rise aloof from these manoeuvres 'creepy to behold',
austere specimens of our American royal families,
'each like the shadow of the one beside it.
The rock seems frail compared with their dark energy of
    life',
its vermilion and onyx and manganese-blue interior
    expensiveness
left at the mercy of the weather;
'stained transversely by iron where the water drips down',
recognized by its plants and its animals.
Completing a circle,
you have been deceived into thinking that you have
    progressed,

under the polite needles of the larches
'hung to filter, not to intercept the sunlight'—
met by tightly wattled spruce-twigs
'conformed to an edge like clipped cypress
as if no branch could penetrate the cold beyond its
    company';
and dumps of gold and silver ore enclosing The Goat's
    Mirror—
that lady-fingerlike depression in the shape of the left
    human foot,
which prejudices you in favour of itself
before you have had time to see the others;
its indigo, pea-green, blue-green, and turquoise,
from a hundred to two hundred feet deep,
'merging in irregular patches in the middle lake
where, like gusts of a storm
obliterating the shadows of the fir-trees, the wind makes
    lanes of ripples'.
What spot could have merits of equal importance
for bears, elk, deer, wolves, goats, and ducks?
Pre-empted by their ancestors,
this is the property of the exacting porcupine,
and of the rat 'slipping along to its burrow in the swamp
or pausing on high ground to smell the heather';
of 'thoughtful beavers
making drains which seem the work of careful men with
    shovels',
and of the bears inspecting unexpectedly
ant-hills and berry-bushes.
Composed of calcium gems and alabaster pillars,

topaz, tourmaline crystals and amethyst quartz,
their den is somewhere else, concealed in the confusion
of 'blue forests thrown together with marble and jasper and
    agate
as if whole quarries had been dynamited'.
And farther up, in stag-at-bay position
as a scintillating fragment of these terrible stalagmites,
stands the goat,
its eye fixed on the waterfall which never seems to fall—
an endless skein swayed by the wind,
immune to force of gravity in the perspective of the peaks.
A special antelope
acclimated to 'grottoes from which issue penetrating
    draughts
which make you wonder why you came',
it stands its ground
on cliffs the colour of the clouds, of petrified white
    vapour—
black feet, eyes, nose, and horns, engraved on dazzling
    ice-fields,
the ermine body on the crystal peak;
the sun kindling its shoulders to maximum heat like
    acetylene, dyeing them white—
upon this antique pedestal,
'a mountain with those graceful lines which prove it a
    volcano',
its top a complete cone like Fujiyama's
till an explosion blew it off.
Distinguished by a beauty
of which 'the visitor dare never fully speak at home
for fear of being stoned as an imposter',

Big Snow Mountain is the home of a diversity of creatures:
those who 'have lived in hotels
but who now live in camps—who prefer to';
the mountain guide evolving from the trapper,
'in two pairs of trousers, the outer one older,
wearing slowly away from the feet to the knees';
'the nine-striped chipmunk
running with unmammal-like agility along a log';
the water ouzel
with 'its passion for rapids and high-pressured falls',
building under the arch of some tiny Niagara;
the white-tailed ptarmigan 'in winter solid white,
feeding on heather-bells and alpine buckwheat';
and the eleven eagles of the west,
'fond of the spring fragrance and the winter colours',
used to the unegoistic action of the glaciers
and 'several hours of frost every midsummer night'.
'They make a nice appearance, don't they',
happy seeing nothing?
Perched on treacherous lava and pumice—
those unadjusted chimney-pots and cleavers
which stipulate 'names and addresses of persons to notify
in case of disaster'—
they hear the roar of ice and supervise the water
winding slowly through the cliffs,
the road 'climbing like the thread
which forms the groove around a snail-shell,
doubling back and forth until where snow begins, it ends'.
No 'deliberate wide-eyed wistfulness' is here
among the boulders sunk in ripples and white water
where 'when you hear the best wild music of the forest

it is sure to be a marmot',
the victim on some slight observatory,
of 'a struggle between curiosity and caution',
inquiring what has scared it:
a stone from the moraine descending in leaps,
another marmot, or the spotted ponies with glass eyes,
brought up on frosty grass and flowers
and rapid draughts of ice-water.
Instructed none knows how, to climb the mountain,
by business men who as totemic scenery of Canada,
require for recreation
three hundred and sixty-five holidays in the year,
these conspicuously spotted little horses are peculiar;
hard to discern among the birch-trees, ferns, and lily-pads,
avalanche lilies, Indian paint-brushes,
bear's ears and kittentails,
and miniature cavalcades of chlorophylless fungi
magnified in profile on the moss-beds like moonstones in
       the water;
the cavalcade of calico competing
with the original American menagerie of styles
among the white flowers of the rhododendron surmounting
       rigid leaves
upon which moisture works its alchemy,
transmuting verdure into onyx.

'Like happy souls in Hell', enjoying mental difficulties,
the grasshoppers of Greece
amused themselves with delicate behaviour
because it was 'so noble and so fair';

not practised in adapting their intelligence
to eagle-traps and snow-shoes,
to alpenstocks and other toys contrived by those
'alive to the advantage of invigorating pleasures'.
Bows, arrows, oars, and paddles, for which trees provide
    the wood,
in new countries more eloquent than elsewhere—
augmenting the assertion that, essentially humane,
'the forest affords wood for dwellings and by its beauty
    stimulates
the moral vigour of its citizens'.
The Greeks liked smoothness, distrusting what was back
of what could not be clearly seen,
resolving with benevolent conclusiveness,
'complexities which still will be complexities
as long as the world lasts';
ascribing what we clumsily call happiness,
to 'an accident or a quality,
a spiritual substance or the soul itself,
an act, a disposition, or a habit,
or a habit infused, to which the soul has been persuaded,
or something distinct from a habit, a power—'
such power as Adam had and we are still devoid of.
'Emotionally sensitive, their hearts were hard';
their wisdom was remote
from that of these odd oracles of cool official sarcasm,
upon this game preserve
where 'guns, nets, seines, traps and explosives,
hired vehicles, gambling and intoxicants are prohibited;
disobedient persons being summarily removed

and not allowed to return without permission in writing'.
It is self-evident
that it is frightful to have everything afraid of one;
that one must do as one is told
and eat rice, prunes, dates, raisins, hardtack, and tomatoes
if one would 'conquer the main peak' of Mount Tacoma,
this fossil flower concise without a shiver,
intact when it is cut,
damned for its sacrosanct remoteness—
like Henry James 'damned by the public for decorum';
not decorum, but restraint;
it is the love of doing hard things
that rebuffed and wore them out—a public out of
     sympathy with neatness.
Neatness of finish! Neatness of finish!
Relentless accuracy is the nature of this octopus
with its capacity for fact.
'Creeping slowly as with meditated stealth,
its arms seeming to approach from all directions',
it receives one under winds that 'tear the snow to bits
and hurl it like a sandblast
shearing off twigs and loose bark from the trees'.
Is 'tree' the word for these things
'flat on the ground like vines'?
some 'bent in a half circle with branches on one side
suggesting dust-brushes, not trees;
some finding strength in union, forming little stunted
     groves,
their flattened mats of branches shrunk in trying to escape'
from the hard mountain 'planed by ice and polished by the
     wind'—

the white volcano with no weather side;
the lightning flashing at its base,
rain falling in the valleys, and snow falling on the peak —
the glassy octopus symmetrically pointed,
its claw cut by the avalanche
'with a sound like the crack of a rifle,
in a curtain of powdered snow launched like a waterfall'.

with their respective lions—
'mighty monoceroses with immeasured tayles'—
these are those very animals
described by the cartographers of 1539,
defiantly revolving
in such a way that
the long keel of white exhibited in tumbling,
disperses giant weeds
and those sea snakes whose forms, looped in the foam,
    'disquiet shippers'.
Not ignorant of how a voyager obtained the horn of a sea
    unicorn
to give to Queen Elizabeth,
who thought it worth a hundred thousand pounds,
they persevere in swimming where they like,
finding the place where lions live in herds,
strewn on the beach like stones with lesser stones—
and bears are white;
discovering Antarctica, its penguin kings and icy spires,
and Sir John Hawkins' Florida
'abounding in land unicorns and lions;
since where the one is,
its arch enemy cannot be missing'.
Thus personalities by nature much opposed,
can be combined in such a way
that when they do agree, their unanimity is great,
'in politics, in trade, law, sport, religion,
china-collecting, tennis, and church-going'.
You have remarked this fourfold combination of strange
    animals,
upon embroideries

enwrought with 'polished garlands' of agreeing
    difference—
thorns, 'myrtle rods, and shafts of bay',
'cobwebs, and knotts, and mulberries'
of lapis-lazuli and pomegranate and malachite—
Britannia's sea unicorn with its rebellious child
now ostentatiously indigenous to the new English coast;
and its land lion oddly tolerant of those pacific
    counterparts to it,
the water lions of the west.
This is a strange fraternity—these sea lions and land lions,
land unicorns and sea unicorns:
the lion civilly rampant,
tame and concessive like the long-tailed bear of Ecuador—
the lion standing up against this screen of woven air
which is the forest:
The unicorn also, on its hind legs in reciprocity.
A puzzle to the hunters, is this haughtiest of beasts,
to be distinguished from those born without a horn,
in use like Saint Jerome's tame lion, as domestics;
rebelling proudly at the dogs
which are dismayed by the chain lightning
playing at them from its horn—
the dogs persistent in pursuit of it as if it could be caught,
'deriving agreeable terror' from its 'moonbeam throat'
on fire like its white coat and unconsumed as if of
    salamander's skin.
So wary as to disappear for centuries and reappear,
yet never to be caught,
the unicorn has been preserved
by an unmatched device

wrought like the work of expert blacksmiths,
with which nothing can compare—
this animal of that one horn
throwing itself upon which head foremost from a cliff,
it walks away unharmed;
proficient in this feat which, like Herodotus,
I have not seen except in pictures.
Thus this strange animal with its miraculous elusiveness,
has come to be unique,
'impossible to take alive',
tamed only by a lady inoffensive like itself—
as curiously wild and gentle;
'as straight and slender as the crest,
or antlet of the one-beam'd beast'.
Upon the printed page,
also by word of mouth,
we have a record of it all
and how, unfearful of deceit,
etched like an equine monster of an old celestial map,
beside a cloud or dress of Virgin-Mary blue,
improved 'all over slightly with snakes of Venice gold,
and silver, and some O's',
the unicorn 'with pavon high', approaches eagerly;
until engrossed by what appears of this strange enemy,
upon the map, 'upon her lap',
its 'mild wild head doth lie'.

❀ The Monkey Puzzle

A kind of monkey or pine-lemur
not of interest to the monkey,
in a kind of Flaubert's Carthage, it defies one—
this 'Paduan cat with lizard', this 'tiger in a bamboo
    thicket'.
'An interwoven somewhat', it will not come out.
Ignore the Foo dog and it is forthwith more than a dog,
its tail superimposed upon itself in a complacent half spiral,
incidentally so witty;
but this pine-tree—this pine-tiger, is a tiger, not a dog.
It knows that if a nomad may have dignity,
Gibraltar has had more—
that 'it is better to be lonely than unhappy'.
A conifer contrived in imitation of the glyptic work of jade
    and hard-stone cutters,
a true curio in this bypath of curio collecting,
it is worth its weight in gold, but no one takes it
from these woods in which society's not knowing is
    colossal,
the lion's ferocious chrysanthemum head seeming kind by
    comparison
This porcupine-quilled, complicated starkness—
this is beauty—'a certain proportion in the skeleton which
    gives the best results'.
One is at a loss, however, to know why it should be here,
in this morose part of the earth—
to account for its origin at all;
but we prove, we do not explain our birth.

❦ Injudicious Gardening

If yellow betokens infidelity,
   I am an infidel.
      I could not bear a yellow rose ill will
      Because books said that yellow boded ill,
   White promised well.

However, your particular possession,
   The sense of privacy,
      Indeed might deprecate
      Offended ears, and need not tolerate
   Effrontery.

❧ To Military Progress

You use your mind
Like a millstone to grind
    Chaff.
You polish it
And with your warped wit
    Laugh

At your torso,
Prostrate where the crow
    Falls
On such faint hearts
As its god imparts,
    Calls

And claps its wings
Till the tumult brings
    More
Black minute-men
To revive again,
    War

At little cost.
They cry for the lost
    Head
And seek their prize
Till the evening sky's
    Red.

❧ *An Egyptian Pulled Glass Bottle*
   in the Shape of a Fish

Here we have thirst
And patience, from the first,
   And art, as in a wave held up for us to see
   In its essential perpendicularity;

Not brittle but
Intense—the spectrum, that
   Spectacular and nimble animal the fish,
   Whose scales turn aside the sun's sword with their polish.

❧ To a Steam Roller

The illustration
is nothing to you without the application.
   You lack half wit. You crush all the particles down
      into close conformity, and then walk back and forth
         on them.

Sparkling chips of rock
are crushed down to the level of the parent block.
   Were not 'impersonal judgment in aesthetic
      matters, a metaphysical impossibility', you

might fairly achieve
it. As for butterflies, I can hardly conceive
   of one's attending upon you, but to question
      the congruence of the complement is vain, if it exists.

❧ *To a Snail*

If 'compression is the first grace of style',
you have it. Contractility is a virtue
as modesty is a virtue.
It is not the acquisition of any one thing
that is able to adorn,
or the incidental quality that occurs
as a concomitant of something well said,
that we value in style,
but the principle that is hid:
in the absence of feet, 'a method of conclusions';
'a knowledge of principles',
in the curious phenomenon of your occipital horn.

❦ 'Nothing Will Cure the Sick Lion but to Eat an Ape'

Perceiving that in the masked ball
attitude, there is a hollowness
that beauty's light momentum can't redeem;
    since disproportionate satisfaction anywhere
    lacks a proportionate air,

he let us know without offence
by his hands' denunciatory
upheaval, that he despised the fashion
    of curing us with an ape—making it his care
    to smother us with fresh air.

❦ To the Peacock of France

In 'taking charge of your possessions when you saw them'
        you became a golden jay.
Scaramouche said you charmed his charm away,
  But not his colour? Yes, his colour when you liked.
  Of chiselled setting and black-opalescent dye,
    You were the jewelry of sense;
      Of sense, not licence; you but trod the pace
      Of liberty in market-place
        And court. Molière,
        The huggermugger repertory of your first
          adventure, is your own affair.

'Anchorites do not dwell in theatres', and peacocks do not
        flourish in a cell.
Why make distinctions? The results were well
  When you were on the boards; nor were your triumphs
        bought
  At horrifying sacrifice of stringency.
    You hated sham; you ranted up
      And down through the conventions of excess;
      Nor did the King love you the less
        Nor did the world,
        In whose chief interest and for whose spontaneous
          delight, your broad tail was unfurled.

❧ The Past Is the Present

If external action is effete
  and rhyme is outmoded,
    I shall revert to you,
    Habakkuk, as on a recent occasion I was goaded
        into doing by XY, who was speaking of unrhymed
          verse.
This man said—I think that I repeat
  his identical words:
    'Hebrew poetry is
    prose with a sort of heightened consciousness.' Ecstasy
        affords
        the occasion and expediency determines the form.

There! You shed a ray
   of whimsicality on a mask of profundity so
      terrific, that I have been dumbfounded by
it oftener than I care to say.
            The book? Titles are chaff.

Authentically
   brief and full of energy, you contribute to your father's
      legibility and are sufficiently
synthetic. Thank you for showing me
            your father's autograph.

❦ Sojourn in the Whale

Trying to open locked doors with a sword, threading
   the points of needles, planting shade trees
    upside down; swallowed by the opaqueness of one
      whom the seas
love better than they love you, Ireland—

you have lived and lived on every kind of shortage.
   You have been compelled by hags to spin
    gold thread from straw and have heard men say: 'There
      is a feminine
temperament in direct contrast to

ours which makes her do these things. Circumscribed by a
   heritage of blindness and native
    incompetence, she will become wise and will be forced to
      give
in. Compelled by experience, she

will turn back; water seeks its own level': and you
   have smiled. 'Water in motion is far
    from level.' You have seen it, when obstacles happened
      to bar
the path, rise automatically.

❦ Silence

My father used to say,
'Superior people never make long visits,
have to be shown Longfellow's grave
or the glass flowers at Harvard.
Self-reliant like the cat—
that takes its prey to privacy,
the mouse's limp tail hanging like a shoelace from its
    mouth—
they sometimes enjoy solitude,
and can be robbed of speech
by speech which has delighted them.
The deepest feeling always shows itself in silence;
not in silence, but restraint'.
Nor was he insincere in saying, 'Make my house your inn'.
Inns are not residences.

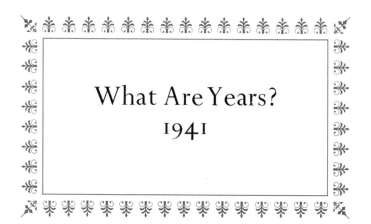

What Are Years?
1941

❧ *What Are Years?*

What is our innocence,
what is our guilt? All are
    naked, none is safe. And whence
is courage: the unanswered question,
the resolute doubt,—
dumbly calling, deafly listening—that
in misfortune, even death,
        encourages others
        and in its defeat, stirs

    the soul to be strong? He
sees deep and is glad, who
    accedes to mortality
and in his imprisonment rises
upon himself as
the sea in a chasm, struggling to be
free and unable to be,
        in its surrendering
        finds its continuing.

    So he who strongly feels,
behaves. The very bird,
    grown taller as he sings, steels
his form straight up. Though he is captive,
his mighty singing
says, satisfaction is a lowly
thing, how pure a thing is joy.
        This is mortality.
        this is eternity.

❦ Rigorists

'We saw reindeer
browsing,' a friend who'd been in Lapland, said:
'finding their own food; they are adapted

to scant *reino*
or pasture, yet they can run eleven
miles in fifty minutes; the feet spread when

the snow is soft,
and act as snow-shoes. They are rigorists,
however handsomely cutwork artists

of Lapland and
Siberia elaborate the trace
or saddle-girth with saw-tooth leather lace.

One looked at us
with its firm face part brown, part white,—a queen
of alpine flowers. Santa Claus' reindeer, seen

at last, had grey-
brown fur, with a neck like edelweiss or
lion's foot,—*leontopodium* more

exactly.' And
this candelabrum-headed ornament
for a place where ornaments are scarce, sent

to Alaska,
was a gift preventing the extinction
of the Esquimo. The battle was won

by a quiet man,
Sheldon Jackson, evangel to that race
whose reprieve he read in the reindeer's face.

❧ Light Is Speech

One can say more of sunlight
   than of speech; but speech
   and light, each
aiding each—when French—
have not disgraced that still un-
extirpated adjective.
Yes, light is speech. Free frank
impartial sunlight, moonlight,
starlight, lighthouse light,
   are language. The Creach'h
d'Ouessant light-
house on its defenceless dot of
rock, is the descendant of Voltaire

whose flaming justice reached a
   man already harmed;
   of unarmed
Montaigne whose balance,
maintained despite the bandit's
hardness, lit remorse's saving
spark; of Émile Littré,
philology's determined,
ardent eight-volume
   Hippocrates-charmed
editor. A
man of fire, a scientist of
freedoms, was firm Maximilien

Paul Émile Littré. England
    guarded by the sea,
    we with re-
enforced Bartholdi's
Liberty holding up her
torch beside the port, hear France
demand, 'Tell me the truth,
especially when it is
    unpleasant.' And we
cannot but reply,
'The word France means
enfranchisement; means one who can
"animate whoever thinks of her." '

❧ He 'Digesteth Harde Yron'

Although the aepyornis
    or roc that lived in Madagascar, and
the moa are extinct,
the camel-sparrow, linked
    with them in size—the large sparrow
Xenophon saw walking by a stream—was and is
a symbol of justice.

This bird watches his chicks with
    a maternal concentration—and he's
been mothering the eggs
at night six weeks—his legs
    their only weapon of defence.
He is swifter than a horse; he has a foot hard
as a hoof; the leopard

is not more suspicious. How
    could he, prized for plumes and eggs and young, used
even as a riding-
beast, respect men hiding
    actor-like in ostrich-skins, with
the right hand making the neck move as if alive and
from a bag the left hand

strewing grain, that ostriches
    might be decoyed and killed! Yes this is he
whose plume was anciently
the plume of justice; he
    whose comic duckling head on its
great neck revolves with compass-needle nervousness
when he stands guard, in S-

like foragings as he is
preening the down on his leaden-skinned back.
The egg piously shown
as Leda's very own
from which Castor and Pollux hatched,
was an ostrich-egg. And what could have been more fit
for the Chinese lawn it

grazed on as a gift to an
emperor who admired strange birds, than this
one who builds his mud-made
nest in dust yet will wade
in lake or sea till only the head shows.

    .   .   .   .   .   .

Six hundred ostrich-brains served
at one banquet, the ostrich-plume-tipped tent
and desert spear, jewel-
gorgeous ugly egg-shell
goblets, eight pairs of ostriches
in harness, dramatize a meaning always missed
by the externalist.

The power of the visible
is the invisible; as even where
no tree of freedom grows,
so-called brute courage knows.
Heroism is exhausting, yet
it contradicts a greed that did not wisely spare
the harmless solitaire

or great auk in its grandeur;
  unsolicitude having swallowed up
all giant birds but an
alert gargantuan
  little-winged, magnificently speedy running-bird. This one
remaining rebel
is the sparrow-camel.

A brass-green bird with grass-
green throat smooth as a nut springs from
   twig to twig askew, copying the
Chinese flower piece,—business-like atom
   in the stiff-leafed tree's blue-
   pink dregs-of-wine pyramids
   of mathematic
   circularity; one of a
   pair. A redbird with a hatchet
   crest lights straight, on a twig
   between the two, bending the
     peculiar
     bouquet down; and there are

   moths and lady-bugs,
a boot-jack firefly with black wings
   and a pink head. 'The legendary white-
eared black bulbul that sings
   only in pure Sanskrit' should
   be here—'tame clever
   true nightingale.' The cardinal-
   bird that is usually a
   pair, looks somewhat odd, like
   'the ambassadorial
     Inverness
     worn by one who dresses

   in New York but dreams of
London.' It was artifice saw,
   on a patch-box pigeon-egg, room for
fervent script, and wrote as with a bird's claw

under the pair on the
hyacinth-blue lid—'joined in
friendship, crowned by love.'
An aspect may deceive; as the
elephant's columbine-tubed trunk
held waveringly out—
an at will heavy thing—is
   delicate.
   Art is unfortunate.

One may be a blameless
bachelor, and it is but a
   step to Congreve. A Rosalindless
redbird comes where people are, knowing they
   have not made a point of
   being where he is—this bird
   which says not sings, 'without loneliness I should be more
   lonely, so I keep it'—half in
   Japanese. And what of
   our clasped hands that swear, 'By Peace
      Plenty; as
      by Wisdom Peace.' Alas!

❧ Bird-Witted

With innocent wide penguin eyes, three
   large fledgling mocking-birds below
the pussy-willow tree,
   stand in a row,
wings touching, feebly solemn,
till they see
     their no longer larger
     mother bringing
something which will partially
feed one of them.

Toward the high-keyed intermittent squeak
   of broken carriage-springs, made by
the three similar, meek-
   coated bird's-eye
freckled forms she comes; and when
from the beak
     of one, the still living
     beetle has dropped
out, she picks it up and puts
it in again.

Standing in the shade till they have dressed
   their thickly-filamented, pale
pussy-willow-surfaced
   coats, they spread tail
and wings, showing one by one,
the modest
     white stripe lengthwise on the
     tail and crosswise
underneath the wing, and the
accordion

is closed again. What delightful note
   with rapid unexpected flute-
sounds leaping from the throat
   of the astute
grown bird, comes back to one from
the remote
      unenergetic sun-
      lit air before
the brood was here? How harsh
the bird's voice has become.

A piebald cat observing them,
   is slowly creeping toward the trim
trio on the tree-stem.
   Unused to him
the three make room—uneasy
new problem.
      A dangling foot that missed
      its grasp, is raised
and finds the twig on which it
planned to perch. The

parent darting down, nerved by what chills
   the blood, and by hope rewarded—
of toil—since nothing fills
   squeaking unfed
mouths, wages deadly combat,
and half kills
      with bayonet beak and
      cruel wings, the
intellectual cautious-
ly cree p ing cat.

❧ *Virginia Britannia*

Pale sand edges England's Old
Dominion. The air is soft, warm, hot
above the cedar-dotted emerald shore
    known to the red-bird, the red-coated musketeer,
    the trumpet-flower, the cavalier,
    the parson, and the wild parishioner. A deer-
track in a church-floor
    brick, and a fine pavement tomb with engraved top,
      remain.
The now tremendous vine-encompassed hackberry
    starred with the ivy-flower,
    shades the church tower;
And a great sinner lyeth here under the sycamore.

A fritillary zigzags
    toward the chancel-shaded resting-place
of this unusual man and sinner who
    waits for a joyful resurrection. We-re-wo-
    co-mo-co's fur crown could be no
    odder than we were, with ostrich, Latin motto,
and small gold horse-shoe
    as arms for an able sting-ray-hampered pioneer—
    painted as a Turk, it seems—continuously
    exciting Captain Smith
    who, patient with
his inferiors, was a pugnacious equal, and to

Powhatan as unflattering
    as grateful. Rare Indian, crowned by
Christopher Newport! The Old Dominion has
    all-green box-sculptured grounds.
    An almost English green surrounds

them. Care has formed among un-English insect
        sounds,
the white wall-rose. As
    thick as Daniel Boone's grape-vine, the stem has
        wide-spaced great
    blunt alternating ostrich-skin warts that were thorns.
    Care has formed walls of yew
    since Indians knew
the Fort Old Field and narrow tongue of land that
        Jamestown was.

    Observe the terse Virginian,
    the mettlesome grey one that drives the
owl from tree to tree and imitates the call
        of whippoorwill or lark or katydid—the lead-
        grey lead-legged mocking-bird with head
        held half away, and meditative eye as dead
as sculptured marble
      eye, alighting noiseless, musing in the semi-sun,
      standing on tall thin legs as if he did not see,
        conspicuous, alone,
        on the stone-
topped table with lead cupids grouped to form the pedestal.

    Narrow herring-bone-laid bricks,
    a dusty pink beside the dwarf box-
bordered pansies, share the ivy-arbor shade
      with cemetery lace settees, one at each side,
      and with the bird: box-bordered tide-
      water gigantic jet black pansies—splendour; pride—

126

not for a decade
   dressed, but for a day, in over-powering velvet; and
   grey-blue-Andalusian-cock-feather pale ones,
      ink-lined on the edge, fur-
      eyed, with ochre
on the cheek. The at first slow, saddle-horse quick
      cavalcade

   of buckeye-burnished jumpers
   and five-gaited mounts, the work-mule and
show-mule and witch-cross door and 'strong sweet prison'
    are a part of what has come about—in the Black
    idiom—from 'advancin' back-
    wards in a circle'; from taking the Potomac
cowbird-like, and on
   The Chickahominy establishing the Negro,
   inadvertent ally and best enemy of tyranny. Rare
     unscent-
     ed, provident-
ly hot, too sweet, inconsistent flower-bed! Old Dominion

   flowers are curious. Some wilt
   in daytime and some close at night. Some
have perfume; some have not. The scarlet much-quilled
    fruiting pomegranate, the African violet,
    fuchsia and camellia, none; yet
    the house-high glistening green magnolia's velvet-
textured flower is filled
   with anaesthetic scent as inconsiderate as
   the gardenia's. Even the gardenia-sprig's

        dark vein on greener
        leaf when seen
against the light, has not near it more small bees than the
        frilled

    silk substanceless faint flower of
    the crape-myrtle has. Odd Pamunkey
princess, birdclaw-ear-ringed; with a pet racoon
        from the Mattaponi (what a bear!). Feminine
        odd Indian young lady! Odd thin-
        gauze-and-taffeta-dressed English one! Terrapin
meat and crested spoon
        feed the mistress of French plum-and-turquoise-piped
            chaise-longue;
    of brass-knobbed slat front door, and everywhere open
        shaded house on Indian-
        named Virginian
streams in counties named for English lords. The
        rattlesnake soon

    said from our once dashingly
    undiffident first flag, 'don't tread on
me,'—tactless symbol of a new republic.
        Priorities were cradled in this region not
        noted for humility; spot
        that has high-singing frogs, cotton-mouth snakes and
            cot-
ton-fields, a unique
    Lawrence pottery with loping wolf design; and too
    unvenomous terrapin in tepid greenness,
        idling near the sea-top;

128

                tobacco-crop
records on church walls; a Devil's Woodyard; and the
                one-brick-

    thick serpentine wall built by
    Jefferson. Like strangler figs choking
a banyan, not an explorer, no imperialist,
        not one of us, in taking what we
        pleased—in colonizing as the
        saying is—has been a synonym for mercy.
The redskin with the deer-
    fur crown, famous for his cruelty, is not all brawn
    and animality. The outdoor tea-table,
            the mandolin-shaped big
            and little fig,
the silkworm-mulberry, the French mull dress with the
            Madeira-

    vine-accompanied edge are,
    when compared with what the colonists
found here in tidewater Virginia, stark
        luxuries. The mere brown hedge-sparrow, with
                reckless
        ardour, unable to suppress
        his satisfaction in man's trustworthy nearness,
even in the dark
    flutes his ecstatic burst of joy—the caraway seed-
    spotted sparrow perched in the dew-drenched juniper
            beside the window-ledge;
            this little hedge-
sparrow that wakes up seven minutes sooner than the lark.

                                        129

The live oak's darkening filagree
of undulating boughs, the etched
solidity of a cypress indivisible
 from the now agèd English hackberry,
 become with lost identity,
 part of the ground, as sunset flames increasingly
against the leaf-chiselled
 blackening ridge of green; while clouds, expanding above
 the town's assertiveness, dwarf it, dwarf arrogance
  that can misunderstand
  importance; and
are to the child an intimation of what glory is.

❧ Spenser's Ireland

has not altered; —
    a place as kind as it is green,
    the greenest place I've never seen.
Every name is a tune.
Denunciations do not affect
      the culprit; nor blows, but it
is torture to him to not be spoken to.
They're natural, —
        the coat, like Venus'
mantle lined with stars,
buttoned close at the neck, — the sleeves new from disuse.

If in Ireland
    they play the harp backward at need,
    and gather at midday the seed
of the fern, eluding
their 'giants all covered with iron,' might
      there be fern seed for unlearn-
ing obduracy and for reinstating
the enchantment?
      Hindered characters
seldom have mothers
in Irish stories, but they all have grandmothers.

It was Irish;
    a match not a marriage was made
    when my great great grandmother'd said
with native genius for
disunion, 'although your suitor be
      perfection, one objection
is enough; he is not

Irish.' Outwitting
      the fairies, befriending the furies,
whoever again
and again says, 'I'll never give in,' never sees

that you're not free
    until you've been made captive by
    supreme belief,—credulity
you say? When large dainty
fingers tremblingly divide the wings
      of the fly for mid-July
with a needle and wrap it with peacock-tail,
or tie wool and
      buzzard's wing, their pride,
like the enchanter's
is in care, not madness. Concurring hands divide

flax for damask
    that when bleached by Irish weather
    has the silvered chamois-leather
water-tightness of a
skin. Twisted torcs and gold new-moon-shaped
      lunulae aren't jewelry
like the purple-coral fuchsia-tree's. Eire—
the guillemot
      so neat and the hen
of the heath and the
linnet spinet-sweet—bespeak relentlessness? Then

they are to me
   like enchanted Earl Gerald who
   changed himself into a stag, to
a great green-eyed cat of
the mountain. Discommodity makes
    them invisible; they've dis-
appeared. The Irish say your trouble is their
trouble and your
      joy their joy? I wish
I could believe it;
I am troubled, I'm dissatisfied, I'm Irish.

❧ Four Quartz Crystal Clocks

There are four vibrators, the world's exactest clocks;
   and these quartz time-pieces that tell
time intervals to other clocks,
   these worksless clocks work well;
independently the same, kept in
    the 41° Bell
      Laboratory time

vault. Checked by a comparator with Arlington,
   they punctualize the 'radio,
cinéma', and 'presse', — a group the
   Giraudoux truth-bureau
of hoped-for accuracy has termed
   'instruments of truth'. We know—
    as Jean Giraudoux says

certain Arabs have not heard—that Napoleon
   is dead; that a quartz prism when
the temperature changes, feels
   the change and that the then
electrified alternate edges
   oppositely charged, threaten
    careful timing; so that

this water-clear crystal as the Greeks used to say,
   this 'clear ice' must be kept at the
same coolness. Repetition, with
   the scientist, should be
synonymous with accuracy.
   The lemur-student can see
    that an aye-aye is not

an angwan-tíbo, potto, or loris. The sea-
    side burden should not embarrass
the bell-boy with the buoy-ball
    endeavouring to pass
hotel patronesses; nor could a
    practised ear confuse the glass
        eyes for taxidermists

with eye-glasses from the optometrist. And as
    MEridian-seven one-two
one-two gives, each fifteenth second
    in the same voice, the new
data—'The time will be' so and so—
    you realize that 'when you
        hear the signal', you'll be

hearing Jupiter or jour pater, the day god—
    the salvaged son of Father Time—
telling the cannibal Chronos
    (eater of his proxime
newborn progeny) that punctuality
    is not a crime.

❧ The Pangolin

Another armoured animal—scale
      lapping scale with spruce-cone regularity until they
form the uninterrupted central
      tail-row! This near artichoke with head and legs and
                  grit-equipped gizzard,
      the night miniature artist engineer is
            Leonardo's—da Vinci's replica—
                  impressive animal and toiler of whom we seldom
                  hear.
            Armour seems extra. But for him,
                  the closing ear-ridge—
                        or bare ear lacking even this small
                        eminence and similarly safe

contracting nose and eye apertures
      impenetrably closable, are not;—a true ant-eater,
not cockroach-eater, who endures
      exhausting solitary trips through unfamiliar ground at
                  night,
      returning before sunrise; stepping in the moonlight,
            on the moonlight peculiarly, that the outside
                  edges of his hands may bear the weight and save
                        the claws
            for digging. Serpentined about
                  the tree, he draws
                        away from danger unpugnaciously,
                        with no sound but a harmless hiss; keeping

the fragile grace of the Thomas-
      of-Leighton Buzzard Westminster Abbey wrought-iron
                  vine, or

rolls himself into a ball that has
   power to defy all effort to unroll it; strongly intailed,
         neat
   head for core, on neck not breaking off, with curled-in
         feet.
     Nevertheless he has sting-proof scales; and nest
       of rocks closed with earth from inside, which he
        can thus darken.
     Sun and moon and day and night and man and
       beast
      each with a splendour
       which man in all his vileness cannot
       set aside; each with an excellence!

'Fearful yet to be feared,' the armoured
   ant-eater met by the driver-ant does not turn back, but
engulfs what he can, the flattened sword-
   edged leafpoints on the tail and artichoke set leg- and
        body-plates
   quivering violently when it retaliates
     and swarms on him. Compact like the furled fringed
        frill
      on the hat-brim of Gargallo's hollow iron head of a
   matador, he will drop and will
     then walk away
       unhurt, although if unintruded on,
       he cautiously works down the tree, helped

by his tail. The giant-pangolin-
   tail, graceful tool, as prop or hand or broom or axe,
       tipped like

the elephant's trunk with special skin,
 is not lost on this ant- and stone-swallowing uninjurable
 artichoke which simpletons thought a living fable
     whom the stones had nourished, whereas ants had
             done
         so. Pangolins are not aggressive animals; between
     dusk and day they have the not unchain-like
             machine-like
         form and frictionless creep of a thing
         made graceful by adversities, con-

versities. To explain grace requires
     a curious hand. If that which is at all were not forever,
 why would those who graced the spires
     with animals and gathered there to rest, on cold luxurious
     low stone seats—a monk and monk and monk—
             between the thus
         ingenious roof-supports, have slaved to confuse
             grace with a kindly manner, time in which to pay
                 a debt,
         the cure for sins, a graceful use
             of what are yet
                 approved stone mullions branching out across
                 the perpendiculars? A sailboat

was the first machine. Pangolins, made
     for moving quietly also, are models of exactness,
 on four legs; or hind feet plantigrade,
     with certain postures of a man. Beneath sun and moon,
             man slaving

to make his life more sweet, leaves half the flowers worth
    having,
   needing to choose wisely how to use his strength;
     a paper-maker like the wasp; a tractor of
      food-stuffs,
    like the ant; spidering a length
     of web from bluffs
       above a stream; in fighting, mechanicked
       like the pangolin; capsizing in

disheartenment. Bedizened or stark
   naked, man, the self, the being we call human, writing-
master to this world, griffons a dark
   'Like does not like like that is obnoxious'; and writes
      error with four
r's. Among animals, one has a sense of humour.
    Humour saves a few steps, it saves years.
     Unignorant,
      modest and unemotional, and all emotion,
    he has everlasting vigour,
     power to grow,
       though there are few creatures who can make
       one
       breathe faster and make one erecter.

Not afraid of anything is he,
    and then goes cowering forth, tread paced to meet an
      obstacle
at every step. Consistent with the
   formula—warm blood, no gills, two pairs of hands and
     a few hairs—that

is a mammal; there he sits in his own habitat,
    serge-clad, strong-shod. The prey of fear, he, always
        curtailed, extinguished, thwarted by the dusk,
            work partly done,
    says to the alternating blaze,
        'Again the sun!
            anew each day; and new and new and new,
            that comes into and steadies my soul.'

❧ *The Paper Nautilus*

For authorities whose hopes
are shaped by mercenaries?
   Writers entrapped by
   teatime fame and by
commuters' comforts? Not for these
   the paper nautilus
   constructs her thin glass shell.

   Giving her perishable
souvenir of hope, a dull
   white outside and smooth-
   edged inner surface
glossy as the sea, the watchful
   maker of it guards it
   day and night; she scarcely

   eats until the eggs are hatched.
Buried eight-fold in her eight
   arms, for she is in
   a sense a devil-
fish, her glass ram's-horn-cradled freight
   is hid but is not crushed;
   as Hercules, bitten

   by a crab loyal to the hydra,
was hindered to succeed,
   the intensively
   watched eggs coming from
the shell free it when they are freed, —
   leaving its wasp-nest flaws
   of white on white, and close-

laid Ionic chiton-folds
like the lines in the mane of
   a Parthenon horse,
    round which the arms had
wound themselves as if they knew love
   is the only fortress
    strong enough to trust to.

Nevertheless,
1944

❧ *Nevertheless*

you've seen a strawberry
    that's had a struggle; yet
    was, where the fragments met,

a hedgehog or a star-
    fish for the multitude
    of seeds. What better food

than apple-seeds—the fruit
    within the fruit—locked in
    like counter-curved twin

hazel-nuts? Frost that kills
    the little rubber-plant-
    leaves of *kok-saghyz*-stalks, can't

harm the roots; they still grow
    in frozen ground. Once where
    there was a prickly-pear-

leaf clinging to barbed wire,
    a root shot down to grow
    in earth two feet below;

as carrots form mandrakes
    or a ram's-horn root some-
    times. Victory won't come

to me unless I go
    to it; a grape-tendril
    ties a knot in knots till

knotted thirty times, — so
    the bound twig that's under-
    gone and over-gone, can't stir.

The weak overcomes its
    menace, the strong over-
    comes itself. What is there

like fortitude! What sap
    went through that little thread
    to make the cherry red!

❧ The Wood-Weasel

emerges daintily, the skunk—
don't laugh—in sylvan black and white chipmunk
regalia. The inky thing
adaptively whited with glistening
goat-fur, is wood-warden. In his
ermined well-cuttlefish-inked wool, he is
determination's totem. Out-
lawed? His sweet face and powerful feet go about
in chieftain's coat of Chilcat cloth.
He is his own protection from the moth,

noble little warrior. That
otter-skin on it, the living pole-cat,
smothers anything that stings. Well,—
this same weasel's playful and his weasel
associates are too. Only
wood-weasels shall associate with me.

❧ *Elephants*

Uplifted and waved until immobilized
wistaria-like, the opposing opposed
mouse-grey twined proboscises' trunk formed by two
trunks, fights itself to a spiraled inter-nosed

deadlock of dyke-enforced massiveness. It's a
knock-down drag-out fight that asks no quarter? Just
a pastime, as when the trunk rains on itself
the pool it siphoned up; or when—since each must

provide his forty-pound bough dinner—he broke
the leafy branches. These templars of the Tooth,
these matched intensities, take master care of
master tools. One, sleeping with the calm of youth,

at full length in the half dry sun-flecked stream-bed,
rests his hunting-horn-curled trunk on shallowed stone.
The sloping hollow of the sleeper's body
cradles the gently breathing eminence's prone

mahout, asleep like a lifeless six-foot
frog, so feather light the elephant's stiff
ear's unconscious of the crossed feet's weight. And the
defenceless human thing sleeps as sound as if

incised with hard wrinkles, embossed with wide ears,
invincibly tusked, made safe by magic hairs!
As if, as if, it is all ifs; we are at
much unease. But magic's masterpiece is theirs,—

Houdini's serenity quelling his fears.
Elephant-ear-witnesses-to-be of hymns
and glorias, these ministrants all grey or
grey with white on legs or trunk, are a pilgrims'

pattern of revery not reverence, — a
religious procession without any priests,
the centuries-old carefullest unrehearsed
play. Blessed by Buddha's Tooth, the obedient beasts

themselves as toothed temples blessing the street, see
the white elephant carry the cushion that
carries the casket that carries the Tooth.
Amenable to what, matched with him, are gnat

trustees, he does not step on them as the white-
canopied blue-cushioned Tooth is augustly
and slowly returned to the shrine. Though white is
the colour of worship and of mourning, he

is not here to worship and he is too wise
to mourn, — a life prisoner but reconciled.
With trunk tucked up compactly — the elephant's
sign of defeat — he resisted, but is the child

of reason now. His straight trunk seems to say: when
what we hoped for came to nothing, we revived.
As loss could not ever alter Socrates'
tranquillity, equanimity's contrived

by the elephant. With the Socrates of
animals as with Sophocles the Bee, on whose
tombstone a hive was incised, sweetness tinctures
his gravity. His held up fore-leg for use

as a stair, to be climbed or descended with
the aid of his ear, expounds the brotherhood
of creatures to man the encroacher, by the
small word with the dot, meaning know,—the verb bùd.

These knowers 'arouse the feeling that they are
allied to man' and can change roles with their trustees.
Hardship makes the soldier; then teachableness
makes him the philosopher—as Socrates,

prudently testing the suspicious thing, knew
the wisest is he who's not sure that he knows.
Who rides on a tiger can never dismount;
asleep on an elephant, that is repose.

❧ A Carriage from Sweden

They say there is a sweeter air
     where it was made, than we have here;
     a Hamlet's castle atmosphere.
At all events there is in Brooklyn
something that makes me feel at home.

No one may see this put-away
     museum-piece, this country cart
     that inner happiness made art;
and yet, in this city of freckled
integrity it is a vein

of resined straightness from north-wind
     hardened Sweden's once-opposed-to-
     compromise archipelago
of rocks. Washington and Gustavus
Adolphus, forgive our decay.

Seats, dashboard and sides of smooth gourd-
     rind texture, a flowered step, swan-
     dart brake, and swirling crustacean-
tailed equine amphibious creatures
that garnish the axle-tree! What

a fine thing! What unannoying
     romance! And how beautiful, she
     with the natural stoop of the
snowy egret, grey-eyed and straight-haired,
for whom it should come to the door, —

of whom it reminds me. The split
   pine fair hair, steady gannet-clear
   eyes and the pine-needled-path deer-
swift step; that is Sweden, land of the
free and the soil for a spruce-tree—

vertical though a seedling—all
   needles: from a green trunk, green shelf
   on shelf fanning out by itself.
The deft white-stockinged dance in thick-soled
shoes! Denmark's sanctuaried Jews!

The puzzle-jugs and hand-spun rugs,
   the root-legged kracken shaped like dogs,
   the hanging buttons and the frogs
that edge the Sunday jackets! Sweden,
you have a runner called the Deer, who

when he's won a race, likes to run
   more; you have the sun-right gable-
   ends due east and west, the table
spread as for a banquet; and the put-
in twin vest-pleats with a fish-fin

effect when you need none. Sweden,
   what makes the people dress that way
   and those who see you wish to stay?
The runner, not too tired to run more
at the end of the race? And that

cart, dolphin-graceful? A Dalrén
    light-house, self-lit?—responsive and
    responsible. I understand;
it's not pine-needle-paths that give spring
when they're run on, it's a Sweden

of moated white castles,—the bed
    of white flowers densely grown in an S
    meaning Sweden and stalwartness,
skill, and a surface that says
Made in Sweden: carts are my trade.

❧ The Mind Is an Enchanting Thing

is an enchanted thing
    like the glaze on a
katydid-wing
        subdivided by sun
        till the nettings are legion.
Like Gieseking playing Scarlatti;

like the apteryx-awl
    as a beak, or the
kiwi's rain-shawl
        of haired feathers, the mind
        feeling its way as though blind,
walks along with its eyes on the ground.

It has memory's ear
    that can hear without
having to hear.
        Like the gyroscope's fall,
        truly unequivocal
because trued by regnant certainty,

it is a power of
    strong enchantment. It
is like the dove-
        neck animated by
        sun; it is memory's eye;
it's conscientious inconsistency.

It tears off the veil; tears
          the temptation, the
mist the heart wears,
          from its eyes,—if the heart
          has a face; it takes apart
dejection. It's fire in the dove-neck's

iridescence; in the
          inconsistencies
of Scarlatti.
          Unconfusion submits
          its confusion to proof; it's
not a Herod's oath that cannot change.

❧ *In Distrust of Merits*

Strengthened to live, strengthened to die for
    medals and positioned victories?
They're fighting, fighting, fighting the blind
    man who thinks he sees,—
who cannot see that the enslaver is
enslaved; the hater, harmed. O shining O
        firm star, O tumultuous
           ocean lashed till small things go
        as they will, the mountainous
           wave makes us who look, know

depth. Lost at sea before they fought! O
        star of David, star of Bethlehem,
O black imperial lion
        of the Lord—emblem
of a risen world—be joined at last, be
joined. There is hate's crown beneath which all is
        death; there's love's without which none
           is king; the blessed deeds bless
        the halo. As contagion
           of sickness makes sickness,

contagion of trust can make trust. They're
        fighting in deserts and caves, one by
one, in battalions and squadrons;
        they're fighting that I
may yet recover from the disease, My
Self; some have it lightly; some will die. 'Man's
        wolf to man' and we devour
           ourselves. The enemy could not
        have made a greater breach in our
           defences. One pilot-

ing a blind man can escape him, but
    Job disheartened by false comfort knew
that nothing can be so defeating
    as a blind man who
can see. O alive who are dead, who are
proud not to see, O small dust of the earth
        that walks so arrogantly,
            trust begets power and faith is
        an affectionate thing. We
            vow, we make this promise

to the fighting—it's a promise—'We'll
    never hate black, white, red, yellow, Jew,
Gentile, Untouchable.' We are
    not competent to
make our vows. With set jaw they are fighting,
fighting, fighting,—some we love whom we know,
        some we love but know not—that
            hearts may feel and not be numb.
        It cures me; or am I what
            I can't believe in? Some

in snow, some on crags, some in quicksands,
    little by little, much by much, they
are fighting fighting fighting that where
    there was death there may
be life. 'When a man is prey to anger,
he is moved by outside things; when he holds
        his ground in patience patience
            patience, that is action or
        beauty,' the soldier's defence
            and hardest armour for

the fight. The world's an orphans' home. Shall
      we never have peace without sorrow?
without pleas of the dying for
      help that won't come? O
quiet form upon the dust, I cannot
look and yet I must. If these great patient
      dyings—all these agonies
            and wound-bearings and bloodshed—
      can teach us how to live, these
            dyings were not wasted.

Hate-hardened heart, O heart of iron,
      iron is iron till it is rust.
There never was a war that was
      not inward; I must
fight till I have conquered in myself what
causes war, but I would not believe it.
      I inwardly did nothing.
            O Iscariot-like crime!
      Beauty is everlasting
            and dust is for a time.

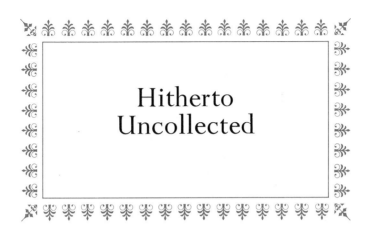

Hitherto
Uncollected

⚘ A Face

'I am not treacherous, callous, jealous, superstitious,
supercilious, venomous, or absolutely hideous':
    studying and studying its expression,
    exasperated desperation
        though at no real impasse,
        would gladly break the glass;

when love of order, ardour, uncircuitous simplicity,
with an expression of inquiry, are all one needs to be!
    Certain faces, a few, one or two — or one
    face photographed by recollection —
        to my mind, to my sight,
        must remain a delight.

✤ By Disposition of Angels

Messengers much like ourselves? Explain it.
Steadfastness the darkness makes explicit?
Something heard most clearly when not near it?
    Above particularities,
These unparticularities praise cannot violate.
  One has seen, in such steadiness never deflected,
  How by darkness a star is perfected.

Star that does not ask me if I see it?
Fir that would not wish me to uproot it?
Speech that does not ask me if I hear it?
    Mysteries expound mysteries.
Steadier than steady, star dazzling me, live and elate,
  No need to say, how like some we have known; too like
      her,
  Too like him, and a-quiver forever.

✾ The Icosasphere

'In Buckinghamshire hedgerows
   the birds nesting in the merged green density,
      weave little bits of string and moths and feathers and
         thistledown,
         in parabolic concentric curves'
and, working for concavity, leave spherical feats of rare
         efficiency;
      whereas through lack of integration,

avid for someone's fortune,
   three were slain and ten committed perjury,
      six died, two killed themselves, and two paid fines for
         risks they'd run.
      But then there is the icosasphere
in which at last we have steel-cutting at its summit of
         economy,
      since twenty triangles conjoined, can wrap one

ball or double-rounded shell
   with almost no waste, so geometrically
      neat, it's an icosahedron. Would the engineers making
         one,
         or Mr. J. O. Jackson tell us
how the Egyptians could have set up seventy-eight-foot
         solid granite vertically?
      We should like to know how that was done.

❧ His Shield

The pin-swin or spine-swine
    (the edgehog miscalled hedgehog) with all his edges out,
    echidna and echinoderm in distressed-
pin-cushion thorn-fur coats, the spiny pig or porcupine,
    the rhino with horned snout—
    everything is battle-dressed.

Pig-fur won't do, I'll wrap
    myself in salamander-skin like Presbyter John.
    A lizard in the midst of flames, a firebrand
that is life, asbestos-eyed asbestos-eared, with tattooed nap
    and permanent pig on
    the instep; he can withstand

fire and won't drown. In his
    unconquerable country of unpompous gusto,
    gold was so common none considered it; greed
and flattery were unknown. Though rubies large as tennis-
    balls conjoined in streams so
    that the mountain seemed to bleed,

the inextinguishable
    salamander styled himself but presbyter. His shield
    was his humility. In Carpasian
linen coat, flanked by his household lion-cubs and sable
    retinue, he revealed
    a formula safer than

168

an armourer's: the power of relinquishing
    what one would keep; that is freedom. Become
        dinosaur-
  skulled, quilled or salamander-wooled, more ironshod
and javelin-dressed than a hedgehog battalion of steel, but be
    dull. Don't be envied or
  armed with a measuring-rod.

✽ 'Keeping Their World Large'*

> All too literally, their flesh
> and their spirit are our shield.
> *New York Times*, 7th June 1944

I should like to see that country's tiles, bedrooms,
stone patios
    and ancient wells: Rinaldo
Caramonica's the cobbler's, Frank Sblendorio's
    and Dominick Angelastro's country—
    the grocer's, the iceman's, the dancer's—the
beautiful Miss Damiano's; wisdom's

and all angels' Italy, this Christmas Day
this Christmas year.
    A noiseless piano, an
innocent war, the heart that can act against itself. Here,
    each unlike and all alike, could
    so many—stumbling, falling, multiplied
till bodies lay as ground to walk on—say

'If Christ and the apostles died in vain, I'll
die in vain with them'?
    When the very heart was a prayer
against this way of victory. Stem after stem
    of what we call the tree—set, row
    on row; that forest of white crosses; the
vision makes us faint. My eyes won't close to it. While

* The Reverend James Gordon Gilkey.

the knife was lifted, Isaac the offering
lay mute.
  These, laid like animals for sacrifice,
like Isaac on the mount, were their own substitute.
  And must they all be harmed by those
   whom they have saved. Tears that don't fall are
    what
  they wanted. Belief in belief marching

  marching marching—all alone, all similar,
spurning pathos,
   clothed in fear—marching to death
marching to life; it was like the cross, is like the cross.
  Keeping their world large, that silent
   marching marching marching and this silence
  for which there is no description, are

  the voices of fighters with no rests between,
who would not yield;
   whose spirits and whose bodies
all too literally were our shield, are still our shield.
  They fought the enemy, we fight
   fat living and self-pity. Shine, O shine
  unfalsifying sun, on this sick scene.

✾ Efforts of Affection

Genesis tells us of Jubal and Jabal.
One handled the harp and one herded the cattle.

Unhackneyed Shakespeare's
'Hay, sweet hay, which hath no fellow,'
Love's extraordinary-ordinary stubbornness
Like La Fontaine's done
by each as if by each alone,
smiling and stemming distraction;
    How welcome:

Vermin-proof and pilfer-proof integration
In which unself-righteousness humbles inspection.

'You know I'm not a saint!' Sainted obsession.
The bleeding-heart's—that strange rubber fern's attraction

Puts perfume to shame.
Unsheared sprays of elephant-ears
Do not make a selfish end look like a noble one.
Truly as the sun
can rot or mend, love can make one
bestial or make a beast a man.
    Thus wholeness—

wholesomeness? best say efforts of affection—
attain integration too tough for infraction.

❧ Voracities and Verities
Sometimes Are Interacting

I don't like diamonds;
the emerald's 'grass-lamp glow' is better;
and unobtrusiveness is dazzling,
upon occasion.
Some kinds of gratitude are trying.

Poets, don't make a fuss;
the elephant's 'crooked trumpet' 'doth write';
and to a tiger-book I am reading* —
I think you know the one—
I am under obligation.

One may be pardoned, yes I know
one may, for love undying.

* Major James Corbett: *Man-Eaters of Kumaon.*

❊ Propriety

is some such word
    as the chord
        Brahms had heard
        from a bird,
sung down near the root of the throat;
it's the little downy woodpecker
           spiralling a tree—
          up up up like mercury:

    a not long
    sparrow-song
        of hayseed
        magnitude—
a tuned reticence with rigour
from strength at the source. Propriety is
        Bach's Solfegietto—
        harmonica and basso.

    The fish-spine
    on firs, on
        sombre trees
        by the sea's
walls of wave-worn rock—have it; and
a moonbow and Bach's cheerful firmness
        in a minor key.
        It's an owl-and-a-pussy-

    both-content
    agreement.
        Come, come. It's
        mixed with wits;

it's not a graceful sadness. It's
resistance with bent head, like foxtail
        millet's. Brahms and Bach,
        no; Bach and Brahms. To thank Bach

    for his song
    first, is wrong.
        Pardon me;
        both are the
unintentional pansy-face
uncursed by self-inspection; blackened
        because born that way.

✤ Armour's Undermining Modesty

At first I thought a pest
Must have alighted on my wrist.
It was a moth almost an owl,
Its wings were furred so well,
with backgammon-board wedges interlacing
on the wing—

    like cloth of gold in a pattern
    of scales with a hair-seal Persian
    sheen. Once, self-determination
    made an axe of a stone
and hacked things out with hairy paws. The consequence—
        our mis-set
alphabet.

    Arise, for it is day.
    Even gifted scholars lose their way
    through faulty etymology.
    No wonder we hate poetry,
and stars and harps and the new moon. If tributes cannot
be implicit,

    give me diatribes and the fragrance of iodine,
    the cork oak acorn grown in Spain;
    the pale-ale-eyed impersonal look
    which the sales-placard gives the bock beer buck.
What is more precise than precision? Illusion.
Knights we've known,

like those familiar
now unfamiliar knights who sought the Grail, were
ducs in old Roman fashion
without the addition
of wreaths and silver rods, and armour gilded
or inlaid.

They did not let self bar
their usefulness to others who were
different. Though Mars is excessive
in being preventive,
heroes need not write an ordinall of attributes to enumerate
what they hate.

I should, I confess,
like to have a talk with one of them about excess,
and armour's undermining modesty
instead of innocent depravity.
A mirror-of-steel uninsistence should countenance
continence,

objectified and not by chance,
there in its frame of circumstance
of innocence and altitude
in an unhackneyed solitude.
There is the tarnish; and there, the imperishable wish.

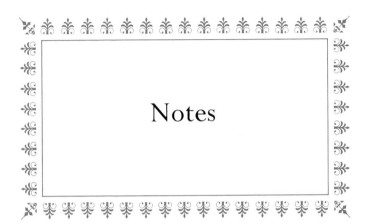

Notes

A *Note on the Notes*

A willingness to satisfy contradictory objections to one's manner of writing, might turn one's work into the donkey that finally found itself being carried by its masters, since some readers suggest that quotation-marks are disruptive of pleasant progress; others, that notes to what should be complete are a pedantry or evidence of an insufficiently realized task. But since in *Observations,* and in anything I have written, there have been lines in which the chief interest is borrowed, and I have not yet been able to outgrow this hybrid method of composition, acknowledgements seem only honest. Perhaps those who are annoyed by provisos, detainments, and postscripts, could be persuaded to take probity on faith and disregard the notes.

M. M.

�֍ Selected Poems, 1935 ✖

THE JERBOA

The Popes' colossal fir-cone of bronze. 'Perforated with holes, it served as a fountain. Its inscription states, "P. Cincius P. I. Salvius fecit." See Duff's *Freedom in the Early Roman Empire.' The Periodical,* February 1929 (Oxford University Press).

Stone locusts. Toilet-box dating from about the twenty-second Egyptian Dynasty. *Illustrated London News,* 26th July 1930.

The king's cane. Description by J. D. S. Pendlebury. *Illustrated London News,* 19th March 1932.

Folding bedroom. The portable bed-chamber of Queen Hetepheres presented to her by her son, Cheops. Described by Dr. G. A. Reisner. *Illustrated London News,* 7th May 1932.

'There are little rats called jerboas which run on long hindlegs as thin as a match. The forelimbs are mere tiny hands.' Dr. R. L. Ditmars, *Strange Animals I Have Known,* p. 274.

CAMELLIA SABINA

The Abbé Berlèse. *Monographie du Genre Camellia* (H. Cousin).

The French are a cruel race, etc. J. S. Watson, Jr.

Bordeaux merchants have spent a great deal of trouble. Encyclopaedia Britannica.

A food-grape. In Vol. I, *The Epicure's Guide to France* (Thornton Butterworth), Curnonsky and Marcel Rouff quote Monselet: 'Everywhere else you eat grapes which have ripened to make wine. In France you eat grapes which have ripened for the table. They are a product at once of nature and

of art.' . . . The bunch 'is covered and uncovered alternately, according to the intensity of the heat, to gild the grapes without scorching them. Those which refuse to ripen—and there are always some—are delicately removed with special scissors, as are also those which have been spoiled by the rain.'
Wild parsnip. Edward W. Nelson, 'Smaller Mammals of North America,' *National Geographic Magazine,* May 1918.
Mouse with a grape. Photograph by Spencer R. Atkinson, *National Geographic Magazine,* February 1932. 'Carrying a baby in her mouth and a grape in her right forepaw, a round-tailed wood rat took this picture.'
The wire cage. Photograph by Alvin E. Worman of Attleboro, Massachusetts, *National Geographic Magazine,* February 1932.

NO SWAN SO FINE
'There is no water so still as the dead fountains of Versailles.' Percy Phillip, *New York Times Magazine,* 10th May 1931.
A pair of Louis XV candelabra with Dresden figures of swans belonging to Lord Balfour.

THE PLUMET BASILISK
Basiliscus Americanus Gray
Guatavita Lake. Associated with the legend of El Dorado, the Gilded One. The king, painted with gums and powdered with gold-dust as symbolic of the sun, the supreme deity, was each year escorted by his nobles on a raft, to the centre of the lake, in a ceremonial of tribute to the goddess of the lake. Here he washed off his golden coat by plunging into the water while those on the raft and on the shores chanted and threw

offerings into the waters—emeralds or objects of gold, silver, or platinum. See A. Hyatt Verrill, *Lost Treasure* (Appleton-Century).

Frank Davis, 'The Chinese Dragon.' *Illustrated London News,* 23rd August 1930. 'He is the god of Rain, and the Ruler of Rivers, Lakes, and Seas. For six months of the year he hibernates in the depths of the sea, living in beautiful palaces. . . .

'We learn from a book of the T'ang Dynasty that "it may cause itself to become visible or invisible at will, and it can become long or short, and coarse or fine, at its own good pleasure." '

A dragon 'is either born a dragon (and true dragons have nine sons) or becomes one by transformation.' There is a 'legend of the carp that try to climb a certain cataract in the western hills. Those that succeed become dragons.'

W. P. Pycraft, 'The Malay Dragon and the "Basilisks." ' *Illustrated London News,* 6th February 1932. The basilisk 'will when alarmed drop to the water and scuttle along the surface on its hind legs. . . . An allied species (Deiropteryx) can not only run along the surface of the water, but can also dive to the bottom, and there find safety till danger is past.'

The Tuatera or Ngarara. In appearance a lizard—with characteristics of the tortoise; on the ribs, uncinate processes like a bird's; and crocodilian features—it is the only living representative of the order Rhynchocephalia. Shown by Captain Stanley Osborne in motion pictures. Cf. *Animals of New Zealand,* by F. W. Hutton and James Drummond (Whitcombe and Tombs).

A fox's bridge. The South American vine suspension bridge.

A ten-ton chain. A seven-hundred-foot chain of gold weighing more than ten tons was being brought from Cuzco,

as part of the ransom for Atahualpa. When news of his mur-
der reached those in command of the convoy, they ordered
that the chain be hidden, and it has never been found. See A.
Hyatt Verrill, *Lost Treasure.*

THE FRIGATE PELICAN

Fregata aquila. The Frigate Pelican of Audubon.

Giant tame armadillo. Photograph and description by W.
Stephen Thomas of New York.

Red-spotted orchids. The blood, supposedly, of natives
slain by Pizarro.

'If I do well, I am blessed,' etc. Hindoo saying.

NINE NECTARINES

Alphonse de Candolle, *Origin of Cultivated Plants* (Apple-
ton, 1886). 'The Chinese believe the oval peaches which are
very red on one side, to be a symbol of long life. . . . According to the word of Chin-noug-king, the peach *Yu* pre-
vents death. If it is not eaten in time, it at least preserves the
body from decay until the end of the world.'

'Brown beaks and cheeks.' Anderson Catalogue 2301, to
Karl Freund collection sale, 1928.

New York Sun, 2nd July 1932. *The World To-day,* by Edgar
Snow, from Soochow, China: 'An old gentleman of China,
whom I met when I first came to this country, volunteered to
name for me what he called the "six certainties." He said:
"You may be sure that the clearest jade comes from Yarkand,
the prettiest flowers from Szechuen, the most fragile porcelain from Kingtehchen, the finest tea from Fukien, the
sheerest silk from Hangchow, and the most beautiful women
from Soochow." '

The kylin (or Chinese unicorn). Frank Davis, *Illustrated*

184

London News, 7th March 1931. 'It has the body of a stag, with a single horn, the tail of a cow, horse's hoofs, a yellow belly, and hair of five colours.'

IN THIS AGE OF HARD TRYING . . .
'*It is not the business of the gods to bake clay pots.*' Turgenev, *Fathers and Sons.*

POETRY
Diary of Tolstoy (Dutton), p. 84. 'Where the boundary between prose and poetry lies, I shall never be able to understand. The question is raised in manuals of style, yet the answer to it lies beyond me. Poetry is verse: prose is not verse. Or else poetry is everything with the exception of business documents and school books.'

'*Literalists of the imagination.*' Yeats, *Ideas of Good and Evil* (A. H. Bullen), p. 182. 'The limitation of his view was from the very intensity of his vision; he was a too literal realist of imagination, as others are of nature; and because he believed that the figures seen by the mind's eye, when exalted by inspiration, were "eternal existences," symbols of divine essences, he hated every grace of style that might obscure their lineaments.'

PEDANTIC LITERALIST
All excerpts from Richard Baxter, *The Saints' Everlasting Rest* (Lippincott).

IN THE DAYS OF PRISMATIC COLOUR
'*Part of it was crawling,*' etc. Nestor, *Greek Anthology* (Loeb Classical Library), Vol. III, p. 129.

PETER
Cat owned by Miss Magdalen Hueber and Miss Maria Weniger.

PICKING AND CHOOSING

Feeling. T. S. Eliot, 'In Memory,' in *The Little Review,* August 1918. 'James's critical genius comes out most tellingly in his mastery over, his baffling escape from Ideas; a mastery and an escape which are perhaps the last test of a superior intelligence. He had a mind so fine that no idea could violate it. . . . In England ideas run wild and pasture on the emotions; instead of thinking with our feelings (a very different thing), we corrupt our feelings with ideas; we produce the political, the emotional idea, evading sensation and thought.'

'*Sad French greens.*' *Compleat Angler.*

'*Top of a* diligence.' Preparatory schoolboy translating Caesar. Recollected by Dr. E. H. Kellogg.

'*A right good salvo of barks,*' '*strong wrinkles.*' Xenophon's *Cynegeticus.*

ENGLAND

'*Chrysalis of the nocturnal butterfly.*' Erté.

'*I envy nobody,*' etc. *Compleat Angler.*

WHEN I BUY PICTURES

Silver fence. 'A silver fence was erected by Constantine to enclose the grave of Adam.' *Literary Digest,* 5th January 1918; descriptive paragraph with photograph.

'*Lit with piercing glances,*' etc. A. R. Gordon, *The Poets of the Old Testament* (Hodder and Stoughton).

THE LABOURS OF HERCULES
'*Charming tadpole notes.*' *The London Spectator.*
'*The Negro is not brutal,*' etc. The Reverend J. W. Darr.

NEW YORK
Fur trade. In 1921 New York succeeded St. Louis as the centre of the wholesale fur trade.

'*As satin needlework,*' etc. George Shiras, Third, *Forest and Stream,* March 1918; *The Literary Digest,* 30th March 1918.

'About the middle of June 1916, a white fawn only a few days old was discovered in a thicket and brought to the hotel. Here, in the company of another fawn, it grew rapidly. During the earlier months this fawn had the usual row of white spots on back and sides, and although there was no difference between these and the body colour, they were conspicuous in the same way that satin needlework in a single colour may carry a varied pattern. . . . '

'*If the fur is not finer,*' etc. Frank Alvah Parsons, *The Psychology of Dress* (Doubleday)—quotes Isabella, Duchess of Gonzaga: 'I wish black cloth even if it cost ten ducats a yard. If it is only as good as that which I see other people wear, I had rather be without it.'

'*Accessibility to experience.*' Henry James.

PEOPLE'S SURROUNDINGS
'*Natural promptness.*' Ward's *English Poets.* Webbe—'a witty gentleman and the very chief of our late rhymers. Gifts of wit and natural promptness appear in him abundantly.'

'*1420 pages.*' Advertisement, *New York Times,* 13th June 1921: 'Paper—As Long as a Man, as Thin as a Hair. One of the Lindenmeyr Lines was selected by Funk and Wagnalls

Company, publishers of *The Literary Digest* and *The Standard Dictionary,* for their twelve-page pamphlet on India Paper. India Paper is so extremely thin that many grew fearful of the results when the unwieldy size, 45 × 65 inches, was mentioned. No mill ever made so large a sheet of India Paper; no printer ever attempted to handle it. But S. D. Warren Company produced the paper and Charles Francis Press printed it—printed it in two colours with perfect register. Warren's India is so thin that 1420 pages make only one inch.'

Persian velvet. Sixteenth-century specimen in the exhibition of Persian objects, Bush Terminal Building, New York City, December 1919, under the auspices of the Persian Throne: 'The design consists of single rose bushes in pearl white and pale black outline, posed on a field of light brown ivory so that the whole piece bears the likeness of the leopard's spots.'

Municipal bat-roost. In San Antonio, Texas, to combat mosquitoes.

Bluebeard's Tower. Bluebeard's limestone tower at St. Thomas, the Virgin Islands.

'*Chessmen carved out of moonstones.*' Anatole France.

'*Like an escalator cut the nerve of progress.*' The Reverend J. W. Darr.

Captains of armies. Raphael, *Horary Astrology.*

SNAKES, MONGOOSES . . .
'*The slight snake,*' etc. George Adam Smith, *Expositor's Bible.*

NOVICES
'Is it the buyer or the seller who gives the money?' Anatole France, *Petit Pierre.*

'*Dracontine cockatrices,*' etc. Southey, *The Young Dragon*.

'Lit by half lights of more conscious art.' A. R. Gordon, *The Poets of the Old Testament* (Hodder and Stoughton).

'The cypress too seems to strengthen the nerves of the brain.' Landor, 'Petrarca,' in *Imaginary Conversations*.

'The Chinese objects of art and porcelain dispersed by Messrs. Puttick and Simpson on the 18th had that tinge of sadness which a reflective mind always feels; it is so little and so much.' Arthur Hadyn, *Illustrated London News*, 26th February 1921.

'*The authors are wonderful people,*' etc. Leigh Hunt's *Autobiography*.

'*Much noble vagueness,*' etc. James Harvey Robinson, *The Mind in the Making*.

'*Split like a glass against a wall.*' *The Decameron*, 'Freaks of Fortune.'

'*Precipitate of dazzling impressions,*' etc. A. R. Gordon.

'*Fathomless suggestions of colour.*' P. T. Forsyth, *Christ on Parnassus* (Hodder and Stoughton).

'*Ocean of hurrying consonants,*' '*with foam on its barriers,*' '*crashing itself out.*' George Adam Smith, *Expositor's Bible*.

'*Flashing lances,*' '*molten fires.*' Leigh Hunt's *Autobiography*.

MARRIAGE

'*Of circular traditions,*' etc. Francis Bacon.

Write simultaneously. 'Miss A—— will write simultaneously in three languages, English, German, and French, talking in the meantime. [She] takes advantage of her abilities in everyday life, writing her letters simultaneously with both hands; namely, the first, third, and fifth words with her left and the second, fourth, and sixth with her right hand. While generally writing outward, she is able as well to write inward with both hands.' 'Multiple Consciousness or Reflex Action of Unaccustomed Range,' *Scientific American,* January 1922.

'*See her, see her in this common world.*' 'George Shock.'

'*That strange paradise unlike flesh, stones,*' etc. Richard Baxter, *The Saints' Everlasting Rest.*

'We were puzzled and we were fascinated, as if by something feline, by something colubrine.' Philip Littell, reviewing Santayana's *Poems* in *The New Republic,* 21st March 1923.

'*Treading chasms,*' etc. Hazlitt, 'Essay on Burke's Style.'

'*Past states,*' etc. Richard Baxter.

'*He experiences a solemn joy,*' etc. 'A Travers Champs,' by Anatole France in *Filles et Garçons* (Hachette): 'le petit Jean comprend qu'il est beau et cette idée le pénètre d'un respect profond de lui-même. . . . Il goûte une joie pieuse à se sentir devenu une idole.'

'*It clothes me with a shirt of fire.*' Hagop Boghossian in a poem, 'The Nightingale.'

'*He dares not clap his hands,*' etc. Edward Thomas, *Feminine Influence on the Poets* (Martin Secker).

'*Illusion of a fire,*' etc. '*as high as deep,*' etc. Richard Baxter.

'Marriage is a law, and the worst of all laws . . . a very trivial object indeed.' Godwin.

'*For love that will gaze an eagle blind,*' etc. Anthony Trollope, *Barchester Towers.*

'*No truth can be fully known until it has been tried by the tooth of disputation.*' Robert of Sorbonne.

'*Darkeneth her countenance as a bear doth.*' Ecclesiasticus.

'*Married people often look that way.*' C. Bertram Hartmann.

'*Seldom and cold,*' etc. Richard Baxter.

'Ahasuerus' *tête-à-tête* banquet.' George Adam Smith, *Expositor's Bible.*

'*Good monster, lead the way.*' The Tempest.

'*Four o'clock does not exist,*' etc. The Comtesse de Noailles, 'Le Thé,' *Femina,* December 1921. 'Dans leur impérieuse humilité elles jouent instinctivement leurs rôles sur le globe.'

'*What monarch,*' etc. From *The Rape of the Lock,* a parody by Mary Frances Nearing, with suggestions by M. Moore.

'*The sound of the flute,*' etc. A. Mitram Rhibany, *The Syrian Christ.* Silence of women—'to an Oriental, this is as poetry set to music.'

'*Men are monopolists,*' etc. Miss M. Carey Thomas, Founder's address, Mount Holyoke, 1921: 'Men practically reserve for themselves stately funerals, splendid monuments, memorial statues, membership in academies, medals, titles, honorary degrees, stars, garters, ribbons, buttons and other shining baubles, so valueless in themselves and yet so infinitely desirable because they are symbols of recognition by their fellow-craftsmen of difficult work well done.'

'*The crumbs from a lion's meal,*' etc. Amos iii, 12. Translation by George Adam Smith, *Expositor's Bible.*

'*A wife is a coffin.*' Ezra Pound.

'*Settle on my hand.*' Charles Reade, *Christie Johnstone.*

'Asiatics have rights; Europeans have obligations.' Edmund Burke.

'*Leaves her peaceful husband,*' etc. Simone Puget, an advertisement entitled 'Change of Fashion,' *English Review,* June 1914: 'Thus proceed pretty dolls when they leave their old home to renovate their frame, and dear others who may abandon their peaceful husband only because they have seen enough of him.'

'*Everything to do with love is mystery,*' etc. F. C. Tilney, *Fables of La Fontaine,* 'Love and Folly,' Book XII, No. 14.

'*Liberty and union,*' etc. Daniel Webster (statue with inscription, Central Park, New York City).

Glass that will bend. Sir William Bell, of the British Institute of Patentees, has made a list of inventions which he says
the world needs: glass that will bend; a smooth road surface
that will not be slippery in wet weather; a furnace that will
conserve ninety-five per cent of its heat; a process to make
flannel unshrinkable; a noiseless aeroplane; a motor engine
of one pound weight per horsepower; methods to reduce
friction; a process to extract phosphorus from vulcanized
india-rubber, so that it can be boiled up and used again;
practical ways of utilizing the tides.

'Picking periwinkles,' etc. M. C. Carey, *London Graphic,*
25th August 1923.

'Spider fashion,' etc. W. P. Pycraft, *Illustrated London
News,* 28th June 1924.

'Ghostly pallor,' 'creeping slowly.' Francis Ward, *Illustrated London News,* 11th August 1923.

'Magnitude of their root systems.' John Muir.

'Creepy to behold.' W. P. Pycraft, *Illustrated London
News,* 28th June 1924.

'Each like the shadow of the one beside it,' etc. Ruskin.

*'Thoughtful beavers,' 'blue stone forests,' 'bristling, puny,
swearing men,' 'tear the snow,' 'flat on the ground,' 'bent in a
half circle.'* Clifton Johnson, *What to See in America* (Macmillan).

'Conformed to an edge,' 'grottoes,' 'two pairs of trousers.'
'My old packer, Bill Peyto . . . would give one or two nervous
yanks at the fringe and tear off the longer pieces, so that his
outer trousers disappeared day by day from below up-
wards. . . . (He usually wears two pairs of trousers).' *Glass
eyes, business men, 'with a sound like the crack of a rifle.'*
W. D. Wilcox, *The Rockies of Canada* (Putnam).

'They make a nice appearance, don't they?' Overheard at
the circus.

Menagerie of styles. W. M., 'The Mystery of an Adjective

and of Evening Clothes,' *London Graphic,* 21st June 1924.

'Greek, that pride-producing language.' Anthony Trollope's *Autobiography.*

'Rashness is rendered innocuous,' '*so noble and so fair.*' Cardinal Newman, *Historical Sketches.*

'*Complexities,*' etc., '*an accident,*' etc. Richard Baxter, *The Saints' Everlasting Rest.*

'The Greeks were emotionally sensitive.' W. D. Hyde, *The Five Great Philosophies* (Macmillan).

Quoted lines of which the source is not given, are from Department of the Interior Rules and Regulations, *The National Parks Portfolio.*

SEA UNICORNS AND LAND UNICORNS

'*Mighty monoceroses,*' etc. Spenser.

'*Disquiet shippers.*' Violet A. Wilson, in *Queen Elizabeth's Maids of Honour* (Lane), quotes Olaus Magnus, *History of the Goths and Swedes,* with regard to the sea serpent; says of Cavendish as a voyager, 'He sailed up the Thames in splendour, the sails of his ship being cloth of gold and his seamen clad in rich silks. Many were the curiosities which the explorers brought home as presents for the ladies. The Queen naturally had first choice and to her fell the unicorn's horn valued at a hundred thousand pounds, which became one of the treasures of Windsor.'

Sir John Hawkins 'affirmed the existence of land unicorns in the forests of Florida, and from their presence deduced abundance of lions because of the antipathy between the two animals, so that "where the one is the other cannot be missing."'

'*In politics, in trade,*' etc. Henry James, *English Hours.*

'*Polished garlands,*' '*myrtle rods.*' J. A. Symonds.

Apropos Queen Elizabeth's dresses, '*cobwebs, and knotts,*

and mulberries.' 'A petticoat embroidered all over slightly with snakes of Venice gold and silver and some O's, with a faire border embroidered like seas, cloudes, and rainbowes.'

The long-tailed bear. In *Adventures in Bolivia* (Lane), p. 193, C. H. Prodgers tells of a strange animal that he bought: 'It was stuffed with long grass and cost me ten shillings, turning out eventually to be a bear with a tail. In his book on wild life, Rowland Ward says, "Amongst the rarest animals is a bear with a tail; this animal is known to exist, is very rare, and only to be found in the forests of Ecuador," and this was where the man who sold it to me said he got it.'

'Agreeable terror.' 'The lover of reading will derive agreeable terror from *Sir Bertram* and *The Haunted Chamber.*' Leigh Hunt's *Autobiography.*

'Moonbeam throat,' 'with pavon high,' 'upon her lap.' 'Mediaeval,' an anonymous poem in *Punch,* 25th April 1923.

An unmatched device. Bulfinch's *Mythology,* under 'Unicorn.'

Herodotus says of the phoenix, 'I have not seen it myself except in a picture.'

'Impossible to take alive.' Pliny.

'As straight,' etc. Charles Cotton, 'An Epitaph on M. H.'

> As soft, and snowy, as that down
> Adorns the Blow-ball's frizzled crown;
> As straight and slender as the crest,
> Or antlet of the one-beam'd beast,

THE MONKEY PUZZLE

The Chile pine (*Araucaria imbricata*). Arauco, a part of southern Chile.

'A certain proportion in the skeleton,' etc. Lafcadio Hearn, *Talks to Writers* (Dodd, Mead).

INJUDICIOUS GARDENING

Letters of Robert Browning and Elizabeth Barrett (Harper), Vol. I, p. 513: 'The yellow rose? "Infidelity," says the dictionary of flowers.' Vol. II, p. 38: 'I planted a full dozen more rose-trees, all white—to take away the yellow-rose reproach!'

TO A SNAIL

'Compression is the first grace of style.' 'The very first grace of style is that which comes from compression.' *Demetrius on Style,* translated by W. Hamilton Fyfe (Heinemann, 1932).

'NOTHING WILL CURE THE SICK LION . . .'

Carlyle, *Letters.*

TO THE PEACOCK OF FRANCE

'Taking charge,' etc., *'anchorites,'* etc. *Molière: A Biography,* by H. C. Chatfield-Taylor (Chatto).

THE PAST IS THE PRESENT

'Hebrew poetry is prose with a sort of heightened consciousness.' Dr. E. H. Kellogg.

'HE WROTE THE HISTORY BOOK'

At the age of five or six, John Andrews, son of Dr. C. M. Andrews, said when asked his name, 'My name is John Andrews; my father wrote the history book.'

SOJOURN IN THE WHALE
'Water in motion is far from level.' Literary Digest.

SILENCE
'My father used to say, "Superior people never make long visits. When I am visiting, I like to go about by myself. I never had to be shown Longfellow's grave or the glass flowers at Harvard."' Miss A. M. Homans.
' "Throw yourself into a coach," said he. "Come down and make my house your inn." ' Edmund Burke, in *Burke's Life*, by Prior.

❧ *What Are Years?* 1941 ❧

RIGORISTS
Sheldon Jackson (1834–1909). Dr. Jackson felt that to feed the Esquimo at government expense was not advisable, that whales having been almost exterminated, the ocean could not be restocked as a river can be with fish, and having prevailed on the government to authorize the importing of reindeer from Siberia, he made an expedition during the summer of 1891, procured sixteen reindeer—by barter—and later brought others. *Report on Introduction of Domestic Reindeer into Alaska*, 1895; 1896; 1897; 1899, by Sheldon Jackson, General Agent of Education in Alaska. U.S. Education Bureau, Washington.

LIGHT IS SPEECH
Creach'h d'Ouessant aeromaritime lighthouse, the first observable—as planned—by ships and planes approaching the continent from North or South America.

A *man already harmed.* Jean Calas, unjustly accused of murdering his son, and put to death, 9th March 1762. In vindicating him and his household, Voltaire 'fut le premier qui s'éleva en sa faveur. Frappé de l'impossibilité du crime dont on accusait Calas le père, ce fut lûy qui engagea la veuve à venir demander justice au Roy. . . .' *The History of the Misfortunes of John Calas, a Victim to Fanaticism, to which is added a Letter from M. Calas to His Wife and Children; Written by M. De Voltaire.* Printed by P. Williamson, Edinburgh, MDCCLXXVI.

Montaigne, captured by bandits and unexpectedly released, says, 'I was told that I owed my deliverance to my bearing and the uncowed resoluteness of my speech, which showed that I was too good a fellow to hold up.'

Littré (1801–1881) devoted the years 1839–1862 to translating and editing Hippocrates.

Bartholdi's Liberty.

'Tell me the truth,' etc. Marshal Pétain.

'Animate whoever thinks of her.' 'Paradise Lost' by Janet Flanner in *Decision,* January 1941.

HE 'DIGESTETH HARDE YRON'

'The estrich digesteth harde yron to preserve his health.' Lyly's *Euphues.*

The large sparrow. 'Xenophon (Anabasis, I, 5, 2) reports many ostriches in the desert on the left . . . side of the middle Euphrates, on the way from North Syria to Babylonia.' George Jennison, *Animals for Show and Pleasure in Ancient Rome.*

A symbol of justice, men in ostrich-skins, Leda's egg, and other allusions. 'Ostrich Egg-shell Cups from Mesopotamia,' by Berthold Laufer, *The Open Court,* May 1926. 'An ostrich plume symbolized truth and justice, and was the emblem of the goddess Ma-at, the patron saint of judges. Her head is adorned with an ostrich feather, her eyes are closed . . . as Justice is blind-folded.'

Six hundred ostrich-brains. At a banquet given by Elagabalus. See above: *Animals for Show and Pleasure in Ancient Rome.*

Egg-shell goblets. E.g., the painted ostrich-egg cup mounted in silver-gilt by Elias Geier of Leipzig about 1589. 'Antiques in and about London' by Edward Wenham. *New York Sun,* 22nd May 1937.

Eight pairs of ostriches. See above: *Animals for Show and Pleasure in Ancient Rome.*

Sparrow-camel: στρουθιοκάμηλος.

SMOOTH GNARLED CRAPE MYRTLE

J. I. Lawrence, *New York Sun,* 23rd June 1934: 'Bulbul is a broadly generic term like sparrow, warbler, bunting. . . . The legendary nightingale of Persia is the white-eared bulbul, *Pycnotus leucotis,* richly garbed in black velvet, trimmed with brown, white, and saffron yellow; and it is a true bulbul; . . . Edward FitzGerald told what Omar meant: that the speech of man changes and coarsens, but the bulbul sings eternally in the "high-piping Pehlevi," the pure heroic Sanskrit of the ancient poets.'

'Those who sleep in New York, but dream of London.' Beau Nash in *The Playbill,* January 1935.

'Joined in friendship, crowned by love.' Battersea box motto.

'Without loneliness,' etc. Yoné Noguchi paraphrasing Saigyo. *The Spectator* (London), 15th February 1935.

'By Peace Plenty; as by Wisdom Peace,' framing horns of

plenty and caduceus, above clasped hands, on the first edition title-page of Lodge's *Rosalynde*.

BIRD-WITTED

Sir Francis Bacon: 'If a boy be bird-witted.'

VIRGINIA BRITANNIA

Cf. *Travaile into Virginia Britannia* by William Strachey.

A great sinner. Inscription in Jamestown churchyard: 'Here lyeth the body of Robert Sherwood who was born in the Parish of Whitechapel near London, a great sinner who waits for a joyful resurrection.'

Werewocomoco. Powhatan's capitol. Of the Indians of a confederacy of about thirty tribes of Algonquins occupying tidewater Virginia, Powhatan was war-chief or head werowance. He presented a deer-skin mantle—now in the Ashmolean—to Captain Newport when crowned by him and Captain John Smith.

Ostrich, horse-shoe. As crest in Captain John Smith's coat of arms, the ostrich with a horse-shoe in its beak—i.e., invincible digestion—reiterates the motto, *Vincere est vivere.*

'Strong sweet prison.' Of Middle Plantation—now Williamsburg.

The one-brick-thick wall designed by Jefferson, on the grounds of the University of Virginia.

Deer-fur crown. 'He [Arahatec] gave our Captaine his Crowne which was of Deare's hayre, Dyed redd.' *Travels and Works of Captain John Smith, President of Virginia and Admiral of New England, 1580–1631;* with Introduction by A. G. Bradley. Arber's Reprints.

The lark. The British Empire Naturalists' Association has found that the hedge-sparrow sings seven minutes earlier than the lark.

SPENSER'S IRELAND

Every name is a tune, it is torture, ancient jewelery, your trouble is their trouble. See 'Ireland: The Rock Whence I Was Hewn' by Don Byrne. *National Geographic Magazine,* March 1927.

The sleeves. In Maria Edgeworth's *Castle Rackrent,* as edited by Professor Morley, Thady Quirk says, 'I wear a long great-coat . . . ; it holds on by a single button round my neck, cloak fashion.'

Venus' mantle. Footnote, *Castle Rackrent:* 'The cloak, or mantle, as described by Thady is of high antiquity. See Spenser's "View of the State of Ireland." '

'The sad-yellow-fly, made with the buzzard's wing,' and 'the shell-fly, for the middle of July.' Maria Edgeworth, *The Absentee.*

The guillemot, the linnet. Happy Memories of Glengarry by Denis O'Sullivan.

Earl Gerald. From a lecture by Padraic Colum.

FOUR QUARTZ CRYSTAL CLOCKS

Bell Telephone Company leaflet, 1939, 'The World's Most Accurate Clocks.' 'In the Bell Telephone Laboratories in New York, in a "time vault" whose temperature is maintained within 1/100 of a degree, at 41° centigrade, are the most accurate clocks in the world—the four quartz crystal clocks. . . . When properly cut and inserted in a suitable circuit, they will control the rate of electric vibration to an

accuracy of one part in a million. . . . When you call MEridian 7–1212 for correct time you get it every 15 seconds.'
'Appeler à l'aide d'un camouflage ces instruments faits pour la vérité qui sont la radio, le cinéma, la presse?' 'J'ai traversé voilà un an des pays arabes où l'on ignorait encore que Napoléon était mort.' Jean Giraudoux, *'Une allocation radiodiffusée de M. Giraudoux aux Françaises à propos de Sainte Catherine.' Figaro,* November 1939.

The cannibal Chronos. Rhea, mother of Zeus, hid him from Chronos who 'devoured all his children except Jupiter (air), Neptune (water), and Pluto (the grave). These, Time cannot consume.' Brewer's *Dictionary of Phrase and Fable.*

THE PANGOLIN
The closing ear-ridge, and certain other detail, from 'Pangolins' by Robert T. Hatt. *Natural History,* December 1935.

Stepping . . . peculiarly. See Lyddeker's *Royal Natural History.*

Thomas-of-Leighton Buzzard vine. A fragment of ironwork in Westminster Abbey.

A sailboat was the first machine. See F. L. Morse, *Power: Its Application from the 17th Dynasty to the 20th Century.*

❀ *Nevertheless, 1944* ❀

ELEPHANTS
Data utilized in these stanzas, from a lecture-film entitled *Ceylon, the Wondrous Isle* by Charles Brooke Elliott. And Cicero, deploring the sacrifice of elephants in the Roman

Games, said they 'aroused both pity and a feeling that the elephant was somehow allied with man.' George Jennison, *Animals for Show and Pleasure in Ancient Rome*, p. 52.

❧ Hitherto Uncollected ❧

THE ICOSASPHERE
'In Buckinghamshire hedgerows,' etc. Statement by E. McKnight Kauffer.
Someone's fortune. The $30,000,000 snuff fortune of a Mrs. Henrietta Edwardina Schaefer Garrett, who died childless and without a will in 1930. 'Orphan's Court, Philadelphia, has reviewed more than 25,990 claims for the fortune. . . . Three persons were reportedly slain in quarrels; ten went to jail for perjury. . . . A dozen or more were fined, six died and two killed themselves.' *New York Times,* 15th December 1949.

'The Mellon Institute is responsible for a steel globe of a design invented by J. O. Jackson, which "solves a problem which has long baffled draughtsmen and engineers. Anybody who has tried to wrap a rubber ball without wrinkling or waste . . . will understand the nature of the problem." Steel, like wrapping-paper, is delivered in rectangles. . . . Mr. Jackson discovered that plexiglass . . . has the same plastic flow as steel and . . . will writhe back into its exact original shape if placed under proper heat. So he moulded a four-inch sphere out of flat plexiglass, studied the pattern and worked out a design whereby "twenty equilateral triangles—the greatest number of regular sides geometrically possible— could be grouped into five parallelograms and cut from rect-

angular sheets with negligible scrap loss." ' Waldemar Kaemf-
fert, 'Economy in the Use of Steel,' *New York Times,* 5th
February 1950.

'KEEPING THEIR WORLD LARGE'

'All too literally, their flesh and their spirit are our shield.'
The Reverend James Gordon Gilkey, *New York Times,* 7th
June 1944.

VORACITIES AND VERITIES . . .

'Grass-lamp glow.' V. Locke-Ellis.
The elephant's 'crooked trumpet doth write.'

> ELEPHANTS
> Yea (if the Grecians doe not mis-recite)
> With's crooked trumpet he doth sometimes write.

Du Bartas, 'The Sixth Day of the First Weeke.'
Dance Index-Ballet Caravan Inc., *Clowns, Elephants, and
Ballerinas,* June 1946.
To a tiger-book. Man-Eaters of Kumaon by Jim Corbett.
With love undying. As the closing words of the sixth chap-
ter of Ephesians, the phrase lingered in my mind. I wrote this
piece, came upon Mr. V. Locke-Ellis' 'grass-lamp glow,' sub-
stituted it for my less good equivalent; upon re-reading his
poems later, I noticed the phrase, 'with love undying,' used by
him also.

PROPRIETY

Bach's Solfeggietto. Karl Philipp Emanuel's (C minor).

Hacked things out with hairy paws. 'The very oldest relics of man's early ancestors are crudely chipped stone. He gripped them in his hairy paw and used them to hammer and chop with.' Oscar Ogg, *The 26 Letters,* p. 6.

Arise, for it is day. The motto of The John Day Company.

The bock beer buck. Poster unsigned, distributed by Eastern Beverage Corporation, Hammonton, New Jersey.

Ducs. 'In England, in the Saxon times, the officers or commanders of armies, after the old Roman fashion, were called *dukes,* without any addition, but after the Norman conquest, the title was no longer used; till, in 1538, Edward III created his son, who was first called the Black Prince, Duke of Cornwall. . . . After Edward the Black Prince, more were made. . . . The Black Prince was created by a wreath on his head, a ring on his finger, and a silver rod.' *The Book of the Ranks and Dignities of British Society,* lately attributed in the press and elsewhere to Charles Lamb (Charles Scribner's Sons, New York, 1924).

INDEX OF FIRST LINES